WHIPPETS TODAY

PATSY GILMOUR

New York

Maxwell Macmillan Canada
Toronto

Maxwell Macmillan International
New York Oxford Singapore Sydney

HOWELL BOOK HOUSE
A Prentice Macmillan Company
15 Columbus Circle
New York, NY 10023

MACMILLAN is a registered trademark of Macmillan, Inc.

Library of Congress Cataloging-in-Publication data

Gilmour, Patsy.
    Whippets today / by Patsy Gilmour. – 1st American ed.
        p.   cm.
    ISBN 0-87605-359-2
    1. Whippets.   I. Title
    SF429.W5G55   1994   94-9843   CIP
    636.7'53 - dc20

Manufactured in Singapore
10 9 8 7 6 5 4 3 2 1

CONTENTS

ACKNOWLEDGEMENTS

Thanks to all the Whippet people who sent in precious photographs – I am sorry that we could not use them all; to Ian Allison (S. Africa), Thomas Munch (Germany), and to Viv Rainsbury for her excellent line drawings.

Special thanks to Harriet Nash Lee for drawing on her unrivalled expertise to provide the chapter on the Whippet in North America, and for the wonderful photographs. Thanks to Gay Robertson for the chapters on the Coursing Whippet and the Racing Whippet, beautifully illustrated by the photographs of Sally Anne Thompson and Ted Walsh. Thanks also to William Dean Wright.

Finally, thank-you to my husband, Danny, for all his help, and to my daughter, Danielle, for being so patient.

Patsy Gilmour.

Chapter One

HISTORY OF THE BREED

Without doubt, the Whippet's rise in popularity took place with the advent of Whippet racing circa 1860. Most of the industrial towns in England and Wales had Whippet tracks, and enthusiasts would meet on a Sunday morning to race, and in the afternoon they would retire to the local hostelry to debate the pros and cons of their respective charges. The sportsmanship of some of these owners may have been debatable, but the honesty of their little dogs had no equal. The charms of the Whippet have melted many a heart, and once you have fallen for this breed, you will want no other,

For its sheer elegance and grace, this great member of the canine race is unmatched – and the sight of a Whippet in full flight is truly awe-inspiring. This small sighthound has an amazing turn of speed, and even as the dog displays such quickness of foot, it is calculating twists and turns, and how long it takes to come to a stop. All this is done in a flash – the Whippet, seemingly, in perpetual motion.

WHIPPET ANCESTORS

There are many theories regarding the genealogical history of the Whippet. Most authorities agree that the Greyhound type is very much to the fore in their make-up. There are theories of the Greyhound being crossed with a terrier and an Italian Greyhound, and of the small Greyhound kept by the Greeks and Romans. Romantic as they sound, I believe the Whippet is more likely to be Celtic in origin. The Celtic tribes in Ireland, who eventually came to Britain, kept all types of hunting and mastiff-type dogs. These great warriors, who were renowned for their love of hunting, both in the forest and in open spaces, were also renowned as great tacticians on the battlefield. This ability was probably learned from watching their hounds take down a quarry on the hunting field. Some of the most beautiful Celtic brooches depict these hunting hounds killing hare and small deer – and all this took place five hundred years before a Roman set foot in England. I personally think that this small hound has come through the centuries, changing and developing, but basically this is the Whippet as we know it today.

Just to put the record straight, there is no doubt that the Greeks and Romans had a small Greyhound. The Greek Pollux, the protector of the hunt, is represented on numerous amphoras (dating from the 6th century BC) with his small Greyhound on some frescos of the classical age. There are also representations of rich Athenians lying on individual

A 'companion dog' taking part in a feast. Corinthian Vase of the 6th century.

couches for communal drinking bouts, and under each couch is tied a dog of the small Greyhound type, wearing a wide, ornate collar.

The Romans also had a great love of the hunting hound. The great Oppian (200 AD), whose work, *Cynegetics*, was to earn him payment of twenty thousand pieces of gold from two Emperors, favours the smaller dog that can run small game to earth. The "vestigator" he says had not the speed of the "vertagus" (little Greyhound). Arrian wrote: "The Gauls of the Cumbri and Celtic tribes have used their hunting dogs from the time of the *Canis Palustris* (Peat Dog), and they (the Gauls) have never ceased to treat them with understanding, gratitude, and friendship."

Indubitably, the Celts and Gauls were masters of what may be called "the canine sport". The quest for meat was no longer the primary aim; this type of hunting was pursued for pleasure. Favourite pastimes were to hunt the stag until it was exhausted, or to capture a hare by letting loose two small Greyhounds at the same moment. "The Gauls," wrote Arrian, "do not hunt in order to capture the game, but to watch their dogs perform with ability and speed. If the hare should escape their pursuit, they recall their dogs and rejoice sincerely in the luck or superiority of the adversary."

The chieftains of Gaul took pains to send the best examples from their packs to their conquerors. For example, Bituit, King of Arverne offered his own small Greyhounds as gifts to the Consul Domitius in 122 BC. So no-one could deny that ancient Gaul had a spirit of generosity and pride in sport – and fifteen hundred years later, hunters and huntsmen of Britain and France still continue this tradition.

Scene of an interior from the Gizimani Breviary (1515), St Mark's Library, Venice.

St. Eustace apearing as a stag to the huntsman. Whippet-type dogs are depicted with their master.

A fine example of Greek ceramic art (433–483 BC).

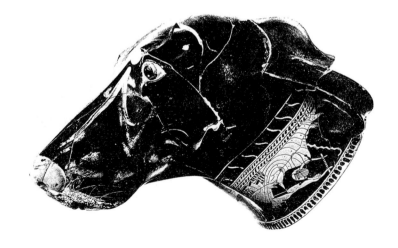

NAMING THE BREED

It has been suggested that the Whippet's name came from the word 'whip' – to stop or crack like a whip – and that the sharp, quick character of the dogs led to the use of the name 'Whippet' or little whip. However, in the *Sportsman's Repository* of 1826 there are several mentions of a breed called a 'wappit', although the descriptions of the breed are very spartan. For example: "Sporting dogs, of which doubtless every farmer desires to possess some, the useful pack upon a farm consists of sheepdogs, rough terriers, vermin curs, and wappits, before all the best guard". Another reference states: "Perhaps a large yard dog should have an attendant of the smaller kind, whence would arise a double security – or a cry of a couple or two of wappits, make an excellent guard, running from place to place and encouraging each other to give tongue and tattle on the approach of a stranger; that they might at the same time well earn their daily bread at the country house as vermin killers." How easily this could be the Whippet!

Portrait of the poet Lamartine, by Decaisne, with his favourite dogs.

Jimanica Jaguar leads Ousebank Sweet Mint on the turn. Coursing was at its height of popularity in the nineteenth century, but the sport still has a strong following in Britain.

E. Walsh.

COURSING DOGS

In the keen coursing days of a hundred and thirty years ago, the standard of height of the dog was, oddly enough, 18 1/2 inches. Just in case the measuring stick does creep back, it is interesting to learn that the bigger dogs were trained at home to pass under a stick with a needle at 18 1/2 inches. Having been pricked a few times, he always managed to get under the Standard. In those days rabbit coursing was the sport, only the kill counting, with none of the refinements of wrench and turn associated with Greyhound coursing. Later the straight run race over 200 yards superseded this. In the Newcastle district the handicap allowance was 8 yards per inch, in South Yorkshire 2 1/2 yards per pound. So that in the North the small dog was the ideal; whereas further south, long thin dogs were favoured.

OFFICIAL RECOGNITION

The Whippet was not recognised by the Kennel Club in England until 1891, and the credit for introducing the first show classes for Whippets goes to Darlington, at the South Durham and Yorkshire Show. The breed gained Challenge Certificate status in 1896. In America, the breed was recognised three years earlier, in 1888, and the first Whippet registered by the American Kennel Club was Jack Dempsey.

In 1895 an attempt was made to free the breed from its association with gaming and to bring it into favour with society. Racing was staged at the LKA Show in Ranelagh Club grounds in the presence of King Edward and Queen Alexandra, but this was not successful. But it was the advent of the Greyhound track and the electric hare in the 1920s, that eclipsed the sport of Whippet racing. Greyhound racing became *the* spectator sport, although there are still hot-beds of enthusiasm for Whippet racing, particularly in the North East of England. In coursing circles, the Whippet is still highly prized, although, again, the more prestigious events go to Greyhounds. However, as a show dog and a companion dog, the Whippet goes from strength to strength. In the USA annual registrations are around 2,000, with litter registrations nearing 500 a year, while in the UK, annual registrations are around 1500.

WCR Ch. Beautiful Venture takes the lead, racing to the finishing line. Whippet racing has been eclipsed by Greyhound racing in terms of spectator support, but the sport still continues to thrive.

Ch. Marshalls Milord at Faracre: The Whippet goes from strength to strength in the show ring.

INFLUENTIAL KENNELS

Present-day success is based on the skill and expertise of breeders from an earlier era, and in Whippets, we are fortunate that some of those doyens of the breed are still with us. The grand old lady of Whippets, Mary Sheffield (Hillgarth), is still attending shows at the age of ninety-five – and still has a keen eye for a good Whippet. Exports from these British kennels have influenced the breed worldwide, and it is worth highlighting the most important prefixes in order to understand the development of the Whippet as a show dog.

LAGUNA

The Laguna kennel, owned by Dorit McKay, is legendary in every country where Whippets are shown. There have been kennels where more Champions have been made up, but never a kennel with such influence. Ch. Laguna Ligonier sired eleven Champions in this country. His most notable sons were Ch. Deepridge Mintmaster, Ch. Towercrest Flarepath Taurus, and Ch. Tantivvey Diver, who was exported to the United States. Mintmaster and Taurus were both very good sires, and Diver sired the lovely Ch. Cockrow Pheasant, and a Champion son, Ch. Fleeting Flamboyant, who went to the famous Whippet breeder, Bo Bengtson in Sweden.

In the USA, Ligonier's son, Ch. Greenbrae Barn Dance, had a record number of Champion progeny, and Laguna Leader was highly successful in Scandinavia. Though of a completely different type, the Dondelayo Whippets all stem from this famous kennel. Ch. Samarkands Greenbrae Tarragon, a son of Ch. Laguna Limelight (out of Ch. Greenbrae Laguna Lucia), and Linknum Star Lizard (by Ch. Laguna Linkway out of Laguna L'Etoile) were the start to this famous dynasty. The Whippet world has so much to thank Dorit McKay and the Lagunas for.

PEPPARDS

Another top kennel I very much admired was the Peppards, owned by Mr and Mrs Gollan. They had many lovely Champion bitches, all homebred, including: P. Faithfull Flora, P. Highland Fling, P. Premium Bond, P. Royal Victory, P. Winterqueen, and the dog P. Topflight. I was lucky enough to come into the breed in the sixties and so I was able to appreciate this lovely bitch-line, and I was lucky enough to own P. Royal Mint, who was the grandmother to one of my favourite bitches, Ch. Solera Scarlet Ribbons at Lowglen.

FLEETING

Molly Garrish also produced many top winners. It was Ch. Fleeting Flamboyant, exported to Bo Bengtson in Sweden, that did so much for the breed in that country. Molly Garrish as a Whippet judge was second to none. She was highly respected the world over.

DEEPRIDGE

Elsie Hawthorne (Deepridge) bred many lovely, quality Champions, and I rate Ch. Deepridge Mintmaster and D. Miniva among the best I have ever seen. She was a very clever breeder, not keeping a large kennel – her Whippets were very much-loved house pets.

SHALFLEET

Barbara Wilton-Clark has spent nearly all her life breeding top-quality hounds, and her Shalfleet Greyhounds are world-famous along with the Whippets. Barbara was a very clever breeder, and the Shalfleet type was unmistakable. She founded her Whippet kennel on the Wingedfoots of Charles Douglas-Todd and the Allways line of Bobby Cooke. These two famous breeders were lucky to have Barbara carry on from where they left off. The Shalfleet kennel had strength in both stud dogs and bitches. They were not flashy, but were entirely to type, and very sound. Their size was as near correct as anything in the ring.

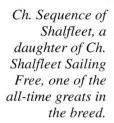

Ch. Sequence of Shalfleet, a daughter of Ch. Shalfleet Sailing Free, one of the all-time greats in the breed.

Thomas Fall.

I rate Ch. Sequence of Shalfleet, a daughter of Ch. Shalfleet Sailing Free, among the all-time greats. She excelled in type. In the late seventies Barbara imported from the Netherlands Ch. 's Silent Knight of Shalfleet, bred by Tim Teillers. He was by the Dutch-bred dog, Dutch Ch. Samoems Scorpion, and his dam, Shalfleet Sylvine, was nearly all pure Shalfleet. He was the first imported dog to gain his title and he proved more than his worth as a stud dog – as did his son, Ch. Shalfleet Silent Wish.

The Shalfleets bred nineteen English Champions and many more overseas.When, due to business commitments, Roger Stock had to disband the Courthill kennel, Barbara kept his bitch-line going for him, enabling him to return to the ring with such success. It was sad when she decided to retire to a warmer climate. Thankfully, we still have her as a highly-respected judge of the breed. The Shalfleets are now in the very capable hands of Cathy Thomas (Faracre). Cathy was left with some very well-bred bitches and Ch. S. Silent Wish. She has carried on in the Shalfleet tradition, making up Ch. Shalfleet Songwriter of Faracre, Ch. Marshalls Milord at Faracre, and the top-winning male for 1993, Ch. Shalfleet Still So Sharp of Faracre – the latter two being sons of Silent Wish. It is greatly to the benefit of the breed that these lines have been kept going.

GLENBERVIE

This kennel, owned by Arthur Badanach Nicholson, produced many lovely bitch Champions founded on the splendid brood bitch, Ch. Hillgarth Sunstar of Glenbervie (bred by Mary Sheffield) and the outstanding sire, Ch. Cockrow Tarquogan of G. (a Tarragon son, bred by the Hudson sisters). The lovely Sky Gypsy of Glenbervie was the start of a long line of Champions for Arthur. This was another kennel whose Whippets were closely line-bred to the great Tarragon. He had great success breeding half-brother and sister.

Ch. Dondelayo Buckaroo, the Tarquogan son, mated to Tarquogan daughters produced many lovely bitches – Ch. Gypsy Picture of Glenbervie, sold to Reg Pye as a puppy, was a perfect example. Arthur sold many good puppies and youngsters on to other people, and many of them became the first Champions for their owners. I feel so lucky to have been able to spend many a Sunday afternoon with Arthur and the Glenbervies when he was at Carnforth. He had a great love for his Whippets and they for him – the Whippets were his family. The Glenbervie affix is now registered in South Africa by Jack Peden (Denorsi). I hope he does justice to this famous name, breeding the quality of Whippets it richly deserves.

COCKROW

The Hudson sisters were very charming and quiet, and I feel that they have not always had the credit that they fully deserved. The Cockrows are behind so many famous kennels and they are a big part of Whippet history. They bred the top producers: Ch. Cockrow Tarragon of Glenbervie, Cockrow Partridge of Crawshaw, Cockrow Grouse, and Cockrow Merle, the dam of Ch. Baydale Cinnamon, another top producer. Out of the Tarragon daughter, Tarradiddle, mated to Ch. Tantivvey Diver came the lovely bitch, Ch. Cockrow Pheasant. They did not overbreed or overshow, but I feel they have done a lot for the Whippet.

DONDELAYO

Anne Knight had kept Whippets for many years before she seriously campaigned them, but she had very well-bred bitches and mated them to very good sires. In 1963 Bill Knight bred John Geary's Ch. Swiftfoot Susannah, and in 1965 Bill also bred what was to be the Meakin's first Champion, Ch. Oakbark Dondelayo Storming. He won his first CC at Manchester under Dorothy Whitwell, and Denis Meakin's now famous trilby hat ended up in the rafters at Bellevue! Both these Champions were by Dondelayo Desperado, one of the few sons of the famous Ch. Courtney Fleetfoot of Pennyworth, both out of daughters of Eng. & Aus. Ch. Playmate of Allways. At this time Anne had the pure Laguna-bred bitch, Linknumstar Lizard, and mated her to the famous Ch. Samarkands Greenbrae Tarragon, and on November 25th 1964 came the start of this famous line with Ch. Dondelayo Rue. Tarragon was line bred for Lizard and was to produce the line of Champion bitches that were to produce Champion after Champion. In 1967 Anne mated Rue to her half-brother Tarquogan, and in this litter came the three Champions: Roulette, Ruanne and the male, Buckaroo. Roulette went on to win Groups and Best in Shows, and for quite a while held the breed record. Buckaroo, the winner of nine Challenge Certificates, proved more than his worth as a sire, going on to sire ten English Champions and many more overseas.

The Dempsters bought Ruanne as a young bitch. She soon gained her title. She was mated twice to Ch. Baydale Cinnamon, a grandson of Ch. Tarragon through his son Ch. Samarkands Sun Courtier. From the first litter came Ch. Charmoll Clansman who quickly gained his title as a young dog. He was exported to the United States where he did so well in the ring and at stud. The second mating produced the two Champion brothers McTavish and Bonnie Prince. McTavish was a prolific sire and produced many Champions and top winners.

It was in December 1969 that another star was born. Roulette was mated to her double grandsire Tarragon and produced the two Champion sisters Duette and Courthill Dondelayo Tiara, the latter being the foundation bitch of Roger Stock's Courthill kennel. Carrying on the tradition of the home kennel, Duette was to win the Hound Group and Supreme Best in Show All Breeds at Peterborough Championship Show 1971. At Crufts 1972 this lovely bitch took the Challenge Certificate and Best of Breed under Ann Argyle. She went on to win the Hound Group and was the first-ever Whippet to win Reserve Best in Show.

Another top bitch from this kennel was Ch. Dondelayo Reinette, a daughter of Ch. Buckaroo and Dondelayo Marianette of Seltaeb, sister of Duette and Tiara. In 1980 Reinette was to win two Supreme Best in Shows at General Championship level – a feat that was not to be repeated for another seven years.

SAMARKAND

Due to Bobby James' heavy schedule as a world-famous international all-round judge, it was impossible for him to breed and campaign his own dogs. Tarragon had already lived with Anne Knight for quite a few years, so it was fitting that his daughter, the famous Duette, was transferred into Bobby's name to keep the Samarkand affix alive. Anne was to breed and campaign Bobby's dogs for him with great success.

The first dog to come out under the Samarkand's affix was S. Sealeopard. He did not do great things in the show ring, but was to prove more than his worth at stud. His litter sister, S. Seamist, was mated to the outcross dog, Ch. Lowglen Newbold Cavalier – one of the few outcross dogs this kennel ever used. From this mating came the youngest dog of any breed to win a Best in Show at a General Championship Show: Samarkand's Skytrain was the tender age of eight and a half months when he took this award at Darlington. He went on to win another CC at Birmingham National, where he also took the Hound Group. Unfortunately, this award was taken away from him as he was entered with his name incorrect. He was never shown on to his title, as he was exported to Australia.

Skytrain's litter sister, Skydrift, was mated back to Sealeopard. Out of this litter came the bitch that was to produce the last crop of Champions for these great breeders – Ch. Samarkand Subaru. This bitch, when mated to Wellnigh Beaubelles (a Sealopard grandson), was to produce Ch. Dyanne Dondelayo, Samarkand Beau Ranger, and Samarkand's Firewolf, plus numerous Champions overseas. Due to Anne's ill health Dyanne went to live with Roma Wright-Smith (Silkstone), who campaigned her with great success and always had her in such pristine condition. In 1986 both Beau Ranger and Dyanne were to qualify for the Champion Stakes finals; Beau Ranger also took the Hound Group and Reserve Best in Show at Welk's Championship Show.

Firewolf was to be the last dog that Anne was to be seen in the ring with. Anne showed so much courage when far from well. She won Firewolf's title and Best of Breed under Humphrey Bradley (1987) at the LKA in an entry of 291 Whippets. However, she was not well enough to take Firewolf into the Group, and so Roma Wright-Smith very kindly stepped in. It was a very sad day for the breed when Anne lost her long fight against illness and died in the Spring of 1988. The whole of the dog world was in great shock when only a few months later her great friend, Bobby James, died suddenly. As a Whippet man he was loved and respected; as an all-round judge he was a legend in his own lifetime.

It was a great loss to the breed that none of these Champions or breeding stock stayed in this country – they were all exported. It was very fitting that Roma Wright-Smith, who had

Ch. Samarkands Beau Ranger, bred by Anne Knight. One of many important Champions to come from this kennel.

done so much for Anne, had bought a puppy out of her last litter. This puppy went on to become Ch. Firedance of Silkstone, a daughter of Firewolf, and the last Champion bred by this great breeder.

ALLGARTH

The Allgarth affix, owned by Frank and Molly Moore, was first registered in 1958, being a combination of Allways and Hillgarth, which was the breeding behind their first Whippets. By the end of 1959 Hillgarth Saucy Sister had been mated to Myhorlyns Shooting Star, and from this litter Allgarth Silver Simon and A. Silver Serenade were retained. Around 1960 a litter was bred by a dog of de Grattan breeding, which produced a litter of puppies either black or white in colour –a lovely quality litter that Frank and Molly were looking forward to showing. Unfortunately, a visitor to the house brought in a distemper infection, and the result nearly wiped out the whole kennel. The litter of de Grattan breeding and a litter by Myhorlyns Shooting Star out of Trixie were all lost. In fact, out of a total of eighteen young Whippets under twelve months, only Allgarth Silver Simon and his sister, A. Silver Serenade, survived. This was a bitter blow, and, but for the late Fred Jones (Allways), who not only consoled them but gave very useful advice and encouragement, the Allgarth line could have ended at this point.

The showing continued with some success, and in due course Hillgarth Saucy Sister was mated to Ch. Fieldspring Bartsia of Allways, and so the Allgarths were picking up the pieces. With Allgarth Silver Simon, Frank realised his early ambitions, for Simon was a superb catcher of hares. His highest total was seventeen hares in one afternoon in a harvest field, and Frank said that he was the best rabbit and hare catcher he ever had. Simon also won well at local shows.

It was in 1967 that Frank bred Allgarth Gemini (by Allgarth Careless Rapture, out of Allgarth Sheena), a silver fawn dog who was the first Allgarth to win the coveted CC. He

Ch. Allgarth Atlantis at Sagewood, a member of a top-class litter whelped by Hound Group winner, Ch. Deborah of Allgarth.

Diane Pearce.

won two tickets, one from Ernest Griffiths (Roanbar), and one from Myrtle Beddall (Myhorlyns). He also won two Reserve CCs, one from Dorothy Whitwell (Seagift) and one from John Owen. He was very unlucky not to gain his title, but Gemini did not enjoy shows and was his own worst enemy. Not disheartened, Frank continued showing and in 1973 he mated Shalfleet Stylish to Ch. Lowglen Newbold Cavalier for the second time, and this time the mating produced the Champions Allgarth Envoy and Allgarth Edelweiss. This litter brother and sister were to win their first CCs under Mary Lowe (Nimrodel) at the Whippet Club of Scotland, where Envoy took the BOB. He won his other CCs from John Owen and Margaret Ironside (Poltesco). With the success of Envoy came offers from abroad to buy him. The most determined, and finally successful, applicants were Brian McCowage and Frank Pieterse in Australia, where Envoy emigrated in January 1976. He had a successful show career, winning his Australian title and several Best in Shows All Breeds. He also made his mark as a sire.

Envoy's departure enabled more time to be devoted to the campaigns of Ambassador of Allgarth (Ch. Flarepath Astrinought of Lowglen) and Deborah of Allgarth (Ch. Lowglen Newbold Cavalier). Ambassador went on to win twelve CCs and twelve Reserve CCs. Deborah won five CCs and five reserve CCs, and she also won the Hound Group at Darlington Championship in 1976. Deborah of Allgarth was mated to Ch. Ambassador and produced a very good litter including Gladys Sage's Ch. Allgarth Atlantis at Sagewood. Top awards and CCs continued to be won by the Allgarths, and Frank and Molly were proud of their record of over twenty-six CCs, thirty-four Reserve CCs, and another six CCs and thirteen Reserve CCs in other ownerships.

In 1982 Frank and Molly went over to Dennis and Dorothy Meakin's Oakbark kennel to look at a litter of puppies by the very successful stud, Ch. Cottonmere Monty of Oakbark, out of the lovely, quality bitch Ch. Oakbark Movie Queen. Frank bought Oakbark May Queen as a present for Molly, and she did quite a lot of winning and picked up a Reserve

CC. May Queen was mated to Ch. Allgarth Atlantis at S. (a dog completely line-bred for her), and in 1985 Molly was to breed her first Champion – not only one, but two in the same litter. They were Ch. Capo Di Monte and Ch. Queen of the May at Marash, who was sold to a newcomer to the breed, Ann Denton. I had the pleasure of awarding this lovely, quality bitch her first CC at the Border Counties Hound Show in 1987, the dog CC going to her litter brother, Ch. Capo Di Monte.

The next litter to be bred by Frank was to be out of an Astrinought granddaughter by Ch. Capo Di Monte, cementing in the very successful combination of Astrinought and Cavalier. Out of this litter came another Champion, Ch. Allgarth Principal, owned by Jill Peak of the famous Bayard Beagles. The other brother, Premier, was kept by Frank. He had won two CCs and several Reserve CCs when Frank suddenly collapsed and died at the beginning of 1990. Like Anne Knight, Frank was to take the CC the last time he was to appear in the ring. It was at Crufts 1989, under Audrey Rolls, with a young bitch he had sold to Gill Peak, Marash Melody of Bayard.

At the time of Frank's death there were many lovely young Whippets waiting in the wings, and I am sure with many more Champions to follow. Sadly, Molly could not carry on with the dogs and many of them were exported, including Capo Di Monte, who joined his litter sister, Queen of the May, in Sweden. It shows what dedication the Moores had for the breed, keeping Whippets for well over thirty years – and a lesson to newcomers that success is not always instant.

Chapter Two

THE WHIPPET PUPPY

CHOOSING A WHIPPET

Numerically, the Whippet is a very strong breed, but it is not – and I hope it never will be – a commercial breed. Most Whippet breeders will only breed a litter occasionally when they require something for themselves. I know, from my own experience, the problems of finding good homes for your pet puppies. The Whippet can make a superb family companion, but this is a breed that requires responsible and caring owners who will understand the whippet temperament.

FINDING A BREEDER

There is no doubt that choosing your first Whippet is a momentous decision for the new enthusiast, whether you want a pet, a show dog, a racing dog, a coursing dog, or a combination of all three. Regardless of the reason why you want to buy a Whippet, you must start with the best possible stock available. Every owner of a pedigree dog wants an animal to be proud of. If you do not know any Whippet breeders in your area, the best course of action is to get in touch with your national Kennel Club. They will supply you with the names and addresses of breeders or those of your nearest breed club secretary, who will always be eager to help the newcomer.

It is generally true to say that the best and most successful breeders have the best stock. They are known for their successes in the show ring, and they are equally well-known for the quality and health of the stock they sell to other breeders and exhibitors. In many cases, these breeders have such a reputation that they will have a waiting list for show puppies and hardly need to advertise. If you are looking for a show puppy, you must be prepared to wait – in the long run it is well worthwhile. In the meantime, you can pass your time learning as much as possible about your new breed. Go to shows where Whippets are scheduled and talk to as many Whippet breeders and exhibitors as possible. You will discover the type of Whippet you like, and you will probably pick up many valuable tips from those who are experienced in the breed.

ASSESSING A LITTER

Most breeders will not let you look at a litter before they are six weeks of age. There are three good reasons for this. Firstly, the dam does not like strangers looking at her new puppies, secondly the puppies need time to build up immunity against disease before they are exposed to visitors, and thirdly, it is between six to eight weeks of age that their individual little characters develop, and they are now relying on the human race rather than the canine. The breeder will not mind you looking at the puppies at six weeks, but a pup should be at least eight weeks of age before leaving the breeder's home. At this stage, the puppies still need individual care and attention, but they are ready to cope with the transition to a new home. A litter which remains a litter too long becomes a pack, and it will be much harder to train the puppies.

The foundation of any good kennel is well-bred bitches, so I always recommend that people start in the breed with the best bitch puppy available to them. You might be lucky enough to be allowed to purchase the pick of the bitch puppies, but remember that the most that can be said about any young puppy is that it is promising. In many a litter, the ugly duckling has turned out to be the swan.

COLOUR
The Whippet can be any colour or mixture of colours. You might have a preference, but at this stage I would not be too influenced by colour. There are not many top Whippet breeders

BRINDLE: Ir. Ch. Mithrandir Panning for Gold.   Dalton.

*FAWN: Ch. Walkabout Waggonerswalk.
                        Diane Pearce.*

*BLACK: Ch.
Laurelcote
Lady In Black.*

WHITE AND FAWN: Barmoll Bedazzled.

BRINDLE AND WHITE: Bohem Wing Commander, owned by Simon Parsons, pictured at 10 months.

BLUE AND WHITE: Ch. Ringmore Thief of Time: The first blue and white particolour in the history of the breed.

who bother about colour at all. You will find fawns, brindles, parti-colours and even black-blues all in the same kennel.

MALE OR FEMALE

You may have decided that, although you would like to show your Whippet, you are not interested in breeding, and a bitch who comes into season every six months might not be suitable for your lifestyle. I find that Whippet dogs are just as lovable as the bitches. Do not believe the old wives' tale that bitches are more faithful than dogs. In fact, I prefer showing males, so it would be far easier to buy a bitch puppy from me than to get me to part with my best dog puppy.

PEDIGREES

Whatever the future may hold for the novice, it is best to start with stock from a well-known kennel where breeding is taken seriously. Pedigrees are all-important, but only insofar as the dogs named in them are known as individuals, with their faults as well as their virtues. A pedigree containing the names of a dozen or more Champions may be of little breeding value though it will look very impressive to a novice.

A pedigree in which the name of a single animal occurs several times, and is famous not only for a show career but also for the merits of the stock he or she has produced, is more likely to produce good puppies than one with a haphazard assortment of Champions, however numerous they have been or famous as individuals.

BEING REALISTIC

The novice who is fortunate enough to start with a first-class animal begins a show career with everything in their favour, but, never forget, even the best of Champions have faults. Always be prepared to learn, and do not expect to go to the top right away. You have chosen a breed that is very strong numerically, and there will always be top-class animals competing. However, you have chosen a very fair breed where the newcomer will never be overlooked – if you have the best animal on the day, you will win. There have been many newcomers to the breed who have made their first Whippet into a Champion.

THE SHOW PUPPY

When you look at Whippet puppies at around the age of eight weeks, they will be starting to take some shape. Do not get the idea that they will look skinny – they should not. Their little bodies should look rounded, with ribs well-covered. Neither the ribs nor the spine should project. The underline should show a slight arch in the loin, although this is not so marked as it will become with maturity. At this stage, the topline – which is such an important feature of the breed – should look fairly flat and long. If a puppy shows too much rise over the loins at this stage, the adult will finish very cut-away.

Most Whippet breeders will have their puppies standing on a table from the age of about five weeks, and by the time they are eight weeks they will be perfect little models for you to look at. The bone should not look fine or fragile. Even at this age, the feet should be tight and well-arched. Thin, poor feet will remain so. When viewed from the front, the front legs should be straight, with the toes turning neither in nor out. When you come to the side of the puppy, the pasterns should show a slight slope, but no sign of weakness. If a puppy knuckles over at the pastern, this will always remain incorrect.

The **elbows** should be well tucked in under the body, and when viewed from the front, you want to see a nice fill between the elbows. If there is a hollow, it is unlikely to alter, and the dog will not have the desired depth of brisket. The straight pastern and hollow chest will usually indicate an incorrect shoulder placement. Tied elbows can also be spotted: the front will look narrow and the toes turn out slightly. The shoulder should be well laid back, and with the correct shoulder you will get the desired length of neck; a short neck also usually indicates a straight shoulder blade.

The **head** should show no signs of apple skull. It should be flat on top and rather wide between the eyes, the muzzle should not be snipey. I think the young puppies with the slight Roman finish will have a good length and strength of muzzle. You also want a good strength of underjaw. A weak underjaw can also indicate that the puppy may finish with the bite being overshot.

The **ears** should be small, rose-shaped, and fine in texture. Although a puppy's ears can look a little large, remember that they do not grow at the same rate as your puppy, and by

A Dumbriton puppy at twelve weeks of age. Note the good bone, tight feet, and good fill in front.

the time the puppy is six months they will look smaller. However, a thick ear will not alter and it may also have a tendency to prick. The **eyes** should be oval, bright, and very alert. The eye-colour depends a lot on coat colour. There is nothing in the Breed Standard stating that the eye should be dark, but puppies with strong pigment usually have little coal-black eyes. **Teeth** are not easy to assess at this age. If the upper lip covers and rests on the lower lip, and the milk teeth are in correct alignment, the permanent teeth are likely also to be correctly aligned.

Regarding the **hindquarters**, the stifles should be well bent. In an eight-week-old puppy I always look for more bend than is desirable in an adult. For, as the puppy grows, the stifle will straighten slightly. If there is not much bend to start with, the pup will finish with hindlegs like pokers. The hocks should be well let down, turning neither in nor out. At this stage, the puppy will not have any muscle on the hindlegs and so may appear a bit unsteady. The tail on an eight-week-old puppy should appear long, sometimes touching the ground. When the puppy is six months, the tail will reach to the hock. It may sound silly, but I always think that quality can show in a tail. A coarse, thick tail usually goes with a coarse animal.

The **coat** should be very soft in texture, fine and bright, never staring, or rough. The skin should be loose and supple. At this stage the dog puppies should look masculine. They should have slightly more bone than the bitches, and the head should look stronger and more masculine. Also check that your dog puppy has two normal testicles fully descended into the scrotum. If there is any doubt at all, ask the breeder to have the puppy checked by a vet before you purchase. It will only lead to heartache later if your promising show prospect is not entire.

Movement at this age is very difficult to assess as Whippet puppies tend to dash hither and thither, never putting all four feet on the floor at the same time. However, if your puppy is correctly constructed, if you take great care with feeding and exercise during the growing period, and the parents are sound, the chances are that your puppy will be sound.

COLLECTING YOUR PUPPY

When the puppy is ready to be brought home, it is advisable to bring along a passenger if you have far to travel, so they can look after the puppy in the car. It is not a good idea to bring a car-load of friends and children, as the puppy will have enough to cope with, without a lot of added stress from too much noise and attention.

Arrange with the breeder the most convenient time to arrive at the kennel. It is better if you arrive fairly early in the day, as this will give your puppy more time to settle once you return home. Do not plan your journey home just after the puppy has eaten, as obviously this will increase the chances of car-sickness. However, you should come equipped with plenty of paper towelling, in case of an accident. You may decide to transport your puppy in a crate, but for this first journey, the puppy will probably be less alarmed if held in a lap.

The breeder will supply you with a receipt for payment, a copy of your puppy's pedigree, and a form so that you can register your Whippet with the Kennel Club. You should also be given a diet sheet, listing what the puppies have been fed and the quantities. You may also be given enough food for the first couple of meals. This is to avoid the possibility of a stomach upset, which can easily happen if the puppy is given different food on top of the trauma of coping with a new home.

CARING FOR YOUR PUPPY

THE RIGHT START

The new puppy is your responsibility, and everything must be done to help the newcomer to settle happily in your home. For a few days, your puppy is going to miss the familiar surrounding of the breeder's home and the companionship of littermates. You must help your new puppy to adapt to the trauma of changing home. Whippets are known for their sweet natures and perfect temperaments, especially with children. But environmental circumstances can deface or destroy a good hereditary pattern. Bad handling, cruelty, neglect, or failure to bring about a happy relationship between dog and human, could all have a great effect on your Whippet puppy. Confidence, once destroyed, takes a long time to re-establish.

BUYING A CRATE

When you buy your puppy, you will make no better investment than a crate. Your puppy will grow to love this little house, and house-training is easier. Equally important, you will not have to cope with the devastation a Whippet puppy can cause when left alone, even for short periods. The puppy can be left in the crate, safe and secure. You can move the crate around the house to whatever area suits you. I have one in the kitchen, and a large one in the bedroom by the radiator. Your cage will fold flat and you can take it to the shows, where your Whippet will feel comfortable and safe.

A crate is an invaluable item of equipment. This twelve-week-old puppy is snuggling up with her grandfather.

ARRIVING HOME

When you first arrive home, give your Whippet puppy a chance to explore. Start off in the garden, in case your puppy needs to relieve itself, and then introduce the pup to the place you have allocated as sleeping quarters. This should be located somewhere that is warm, quiet, and draught-free. It is important to establish, right from the beginning, that this is a place of 'safe haven' for your puppy. All dogs need a place of their own, to rest undisturbed, and as soon as your puppy learns where this is, the sooner you will have a settled puppy.

There are plenty of different types of dog bed to choose from. In this first few weeks, a cardboard box, lined with some soft bedding, will be quite suitable. It does not matter if it is chewed, and you can replace it with a bigger box, as your puppy grows. When you decide to buy a bed, you will probably finds that the plastic, kidney-shaped dog-beds are the most durable, and they have the advantage of being easy to clean.

In the US, crates are a standard item of equipment, and they are becoming increasingly popular in the UK. They provide a safe and secure place to confine your puppy for short periods, and they can also be used in the car. Most dogs will happily retire to their crate when the door is left open, and do not view it as an unwelcome restriction on their freedom.

Do not overwhelm your new puppy by filling the house with friends and relations, all wanting to inspect your new arrival. Just give your puppy a chance to get used to the surroundings with as little fuss as possible. Do not be surprised if your puppy refuses the first meal you offer. There is so much to get used to: food – at this moment – may seem of little importance. A healthy puppy will soon make up for missing a meal the next time food is offered.

THE FIRST NIGHT

There are few puppies who get through their first night without some barking and crying.

This is almost certainly the first time your puppy has had to sleep alone, without the warmth and comfort of littermates. It may help if your provide an old soft toy – nothing with eyes and noses that can be chewed off – and this will give your puppy something to snuggle up to. If your puppy cries during the night, try to resist the temptation of giving in. Once a Whippet comes into your bed, you will have a bedmate for life!

HOUSE-TRAINING

House-training a puppy usually takes priority over everything else, and if it is approached in the right way, it should present no difficulty. The length of time it takes to get a puppy house-trained is governed by the time of year and the age of the dog, as well as by the patience and perseverance of the trainer.

Obviously it is not practical to put a Whippet puppy out of doors in very cold weather. Under such conditions, it is much better to teach the puppy to be paper-trained. Start by placing the some newspaper near the door, then as the weather improves, place the paper just outside the door. Gradually substitute a whole double sheet of newspaper for a small piece, and do away with it altogether when the puppy learns to use the same spot outside the house.

One advantage of owning a dog the size of a Whippet is that if your puppy does make a mistake on the carpet, it will not be a big puddle and little damage is done. Most of the liquid detergents are excellent for removing tell-tale puppy stains. For rapid 'first aid', paper tissues and paper towels should be kept on hand. The dry carpet cleaners are also helpful in keeping the carpet fresh-smelling, after you have cleaned up after your puppy.

The younger the puppy, the longer it will be before you can expect your pup to be completely reliable, day and night. This is as much a question of the puppy being physically mature enough to control both bowel and bladder, as of the effectiveness of your training. It is unfair to expect a puppy to go for long periods without making a mess, but as the training sinks in and the pup understands what is required, then it will not be long before you have a fully house-trained dog.

If the weather is reasonably good, then the puppy can be put out in the garden, but you must stay in attendance. It is no use trying to train your puppy to be clean unless you take the time to supervise the garden outings, so that the puppy learns what is required. Otherwise, as far as the puppy is concerned, the warm, dry carpet in the house seems a far more comfortable place for toileting purposes than the damp grass.

Some owners find it useful to use a command, such as "Hurry up" or "Be clean", to encourage the puppy to perform – it is not long before the pup associates the command with the correct action. As soon as your puppy responds, do not forget to give plenty of praise. To begin with, the puppy is unlikely to understand what is wanted. It helps if you take your puppy outside at the right moment – after a meal, after waking from a nap, or when the pup begins to run round the room sniffing at the floor. So pick a likely time, and even if it is boring and chilly, you must hang about for a few minutes so that, with luck, the puppy can be petted, praised, and congratulated before coming back into the house.

Mistakes are inevitable in the early stages of house-training – and you must respond firmly, but never harshly. Take the puppy to the spot, hold the scruff of the neck, and say

"No" in a firm tone of voice. Then carry the puppy to the newspaper you have left out, or to the spot in the garden you have allocated, and wait for a minute or two. Whippets are the most sensitive of creatures. They thrive on love and long to be cradled in affection. Nothing makes them more wretched than to know they have fallen from grace. If someone is cross they will mope and pine, perhaps refuse food, and look utterly pathetic until a change in tone of voice, or a caress, tells them they are forgiven. Then their whole demeanour changes – they become sprightly and happy again.

It is scarcely ever necessary or even wise to smack a Whippet. Just the unsympathetic touch of the hand that grips them, the angry tone of voice is sufficient punishment. The dog knows at once that you are displeased, and begins to reason why. Never attempt to house-train more than one puppy at a time. Many people do make this mistake, and then you hear a wail to the effect that Whippets are hard to house-train. This is not true. They are naturally clean and fastidious. Once trained, the bitches are scarcely ever dirty, and if a male should forget himself, it is generally only if a new bitch, or a bitch in season, has been around and taken his mind off his good manners. Many Whippets of both sexes will suffer discomfort for fear of soiling the wrong place.

The trouble with two or more puppies is that it is difficult to keep a wary eye on more than one at a time. If the puppies are running about, there is sure to be an accident sooner or later, and then it is impossible to identify the culprit. It would be cruel to scold the lot when only one has been naughty, so the offence has to be overlooked. The little criminal finds that crime pays and will be smart enough to do it again.

As puppies cannot be expected to be clean for long periods, some arrangement must be made for the night hours or if it is necessary to leave them unattended for any length of time during the day. It is best to fix up some kind of pen or crate, with the floor space covered with newspapers, which can be easily rolled up and burned. In general, puppies will not soil their beds if they can help it. However, accidents do happen, so it is as well to provide bedding that is easy to dispose of, or easy to wash. It is a mistake to give a puppy an elaborate cushion, or mattress, and even large rugs or blankets are tiresome to wash.

Contact with the puppy should soon show an observant and intelligent owner that the pup is beginning to understand what is required, and it is easy to know when the dog has a clear idea of right and wrong. Similarly, constant association with a puppy should give the owner a 'sixth sense', enabling the puppy's wants to be anticipated. In this way, the owner should be able to decide when the dog can be reasonably expected to stay clean all night, or for longer spells during daytime. Then the little dog can be trusted to be allowed to sleep in a bedroom or sitting-room without being confined to a pen or a crate. Your Whippet will learn to ask to be let out, and you can afford to relax your vigilance, as your dog is now fully house-trained.

FEEDING
It is a good idea to feed the same food the breeder has been providing, for at least the first week after your puppy arrives home. The details of the breeder's chosen diet will be set out in a diet sheet, and you will be given a copy of this when you collect your puppy. Whether you decide to feed a different diet, in due course, is largely a matter of choice (see Chapter

Breeding from top-quality Whippets coupled with good rearing are the key ingredients to success in the show ring. Pictured left to right: Am. Ch. Saxon Shore Flashback, Am. Ch. Saxon Shore Flash Jordan, Am. Ch. Saxon Shore Flashing Lights and Am. Ch. Saxon Shore Flash Point – four of six Champions from a litter by Am. Ch. Delacreme de las Renta ROMX and Am. Ch. Saxon Shore Flash Dance.   *Missy Yuhl.*

Three: The Adult Whippet), but there are a few guidelines which it may be useful to bear in mind. If you are feeding a traditional meat and biscuit diet, meat should be minced or finely chopped. Biscuit meals should be of the puppy size. Many dog food manufacturers produce a specially formulated puppy diet, and you may decide to opt for this while your puppy is growing. Most breeders feed four meals a day to a fully weaned puppy, and I think this is sufficient, especially for breeds in which large bone and size are undesirable.

There is no rule about actual feeding times. They should be fitted into the routine of kennels and household alike. The main thing to remember is that the timetable should be arranged and then every effort made to keep to it. Puppies appreciate punctual meals and do not thrive when fed at odd hours. It is best to space the feeds, so that they do not come too close together. Suggested times are:

8 a.m.: milk and cereal
12 noon: meat meal
4 p.m.: milk and cereal
9 p.m.: meat meal.

The first feed could be goat's milk mixed with cornflakes or porridge. Remember only give goat's milk, as it is wonderful for dogs and a great replacement for their mother's milk. A bit of fish in the main meal can also be beneficial. You can also feed a good-quality biscuit or some brown bread soaked in broth.

The rough guide to quantity should be about the size of the puppy's head for each meal. This is quite sufficient, but some people get very worried because they think their puppy is not eating enough! Others go to the other extreme and feed too much. In this situation, commonsense is essential. If the puppy cleans the dish, looks distended, grunts, whines and runs around in circles, you have given too much to eat, and the puppy is feeling very uncomfortable. If, after gobbling all the food, the puppy looks no fatter and keeps sniffing around hopefully for more, increase the quantity.

As the puppy grows up, keep a sharp watch on overall condition. A Whippet puppy should be well covered with a soft pliable 'flesh'. The muscle and hard solid flesh we like to see in the older Whippet is not right for a puppy, which should be well covered, but not fat. A lean, skinny puppy has nothing in hand if an indisposition, or any other setback, comes along. We know that in a breed like Whippets, many a beautiful puppy has been lost by poor nourishment. Always remember that the puppy is totally dependent on you.

The other danger to avoid is the owner who, with the best intentions, is anxious to give their dog the best of everything, and, fearful lest they stint them of something, they provide calcium supplements, tonics, and every kind of proprietary conditioner. Such things are not necessary. They are best avoided, unless you are acting under the guidance of a veterinary surgeon.

As the puppy gets older, more food is required, but at less frequent intervals. In fact, your puppy will often decide which meal to drop, and as soon as food is being left, you will know that this meal is no longer necessary. The puppy will go from greeting the food with great enthusiasm on every occasion, to consuming one meal but seeming disinterested with the next. This is a sign that their timetable should be condensed and it might be a good idea to stop one of the milk feeds, usually supper. Later still, combine the main meal into one solid dinner, but keep offering the milk breakfast until the puppy rejects it. This usually happens when the dog is nine or ten months of age. From this stage onwards, you can consider your Whippet as an adult, and feed accordingly.

Chapter Three

THE ADULT WHIPPET

GENERAL CARE

Whippets are the perfect house dogs. They are clean, medium-sized, and the most devoted companions. They should never be kennel dogs in the general sense of the word – especially if the kennel is an outside building, usually made of wood, and not warmed or even insulated. Whippets do not thrive in such houses. The breed, unquestionably, does best indoors. Whippets are such individual little dogs; they are so attached to the person who cares for them, and their intelligence develops and blossoms when they have constant human companionship. There can be no question that a house dog's life is every Whippet's vocation.

If an individual is keeping one or two Whippets, there is surely no need to consider keeping them anywhere other than indoors, and most people who keep a small number for breeding and showing generally manage to house them the same way. Though not habitual barkers, Whippets are splendid 'burglar alarms' and as such they are invaluable inside the house. Once the stock increases, a different problem presents itself, and many breeders have attempted to find a solution that the dogs will be reasonably happy with.

ESTABLISHING A ROUTINE

The management of the Whippet, whether it is one house dog or a sizeable kennel, is much the same as the routines recommended for any other breed, in this instance following the lines found suitable for other members of the smaller type of hound. If you are keeping one or two companion dogs, they will be required to fit in with the rest of the household, and their timetable will be established accordingly. However, it is essential that once this schedule is set, you stick to it as closely as possible. It does not matter what time you feed your dogs, or what time you exercise them, so long as you establish a regular routine. This is even more important for dogs who are housed in kennels. A dog who knows what to expect will be far more settled and more content in everyday life.

THE DAILY REGIME

Over the years, I have established a routine which suits my dogs, and it can be tailored to suit the individual's requirements. The dogs have the maximum amount of contact with

Whippets thrive on human companionship, and they are best-suited to being kept as house dogs.

people, and observation is a key word in the general care of the dogs. If you notice what is going on around you, you will notice any small changes in the dog's general well-being. This can be invaluable, for if you spot a problem at an early stage, the chances are that you will be able to solve it relatively easily.

Adult dogs should be put into the garden before breakfast. If there is no garden, the dog must be taken out on a lead. In either case, do not let a Whippet stay out long enough to catch cold, especially if the dog has just come out of a warm sleeping box or from the underside of someone's quilt. As soon as your Whippet has 'performed', you can go back inside. Whippets learn to oblige very rapidly since they dislike being out in the cold. If the owner watches them while they are outside, it is a very good way of checking for loose stools or constipated dogs, so that any problems can be dealt with promptly.

In mild weather, Whippets will enjoy romping in the garden or in a large enclosure, and while they are exercising, their pens can be cleaned, and if you have any puppies, you will need to feed them breakfast. Beds should be taken out and aired, blankets should be well shaken, and the boxes brushed out with a small stiff hand-brush. Any soiled blankets should be put into a washing-machine, dirty boxes should be well scrubbed and left to dry in the sun, and thoroughly aired.

A bucket and shovel, with a small stiff brush (not the one you use for the beds) should be used for going over the surface of the run, or the part of the garden where the dogs are exercised. Remove stools and urine, and take it away to be burned or buried. This is a most important part of kennel routine, and yet, oddly enough, one that is often neglected. Careful attention to this helps to prevent worm infestation, and can prevent more serious illness and infections. Grass, gravel and concrete can get into a disgusting state if it is not given regular bucket-and-shovel drill. In long spells of dry weather, it is nearly always necessary to swill down concrete with buckets of water and disinfectant, and to soak other surfaces with a watering-can fitted with a spray.

A word about disinfectants. There are dozens of brands, some derived from tar, others with a pine-oil base. While they are all effective as a deodorant, some are not quite so efficient as germ-killers. However, most well-known manufacturers make products which conform to a standard, and so the choice really resolves itself into a preference for one particular fragrance. Most veterinary surgeons will tell you that hot water containing some household bleach is the best possible disinfectant, but most people like to use something with a pleasant aroma. Bleach should be used in small proportions, and these proportions should be one-hundredth to each bucket of water. Very strong solutions are no more effective than the correct but weaker strengths, and they can be over-powering if used indoors. After kennel and runs are spick and span, water bowls must be rinsed, wiped out and refilled. Whippets drink very little water, but they like to have it within reach when they do feel thirsty. During summer, drinking vessels should be placed in shady spots, and water must be changed two or three times daily. Bitches in season, bitches with litters, or any other dog confined to the pen, should have individual bowls of clean water so that they can help themselves.

CHECKING YOUR DOG

All the time the kennel work is in progress, the dogs will be running about or sunning themselves outside. Once everything is done, call one dog in at a time for a thorough check-over. This is the time to spot any minor problems, such as bareness on the ears, skull or hock, eyes that require bathing, or teeth that need attention.

The coat should be roughed up the wrong way a few times, so that if the dog has collected a flea from the grass, it is immediately detected. It can be removed with a fine-tooth comb or, with a little practice, a nimble finger and thumb. There is nothing shameful in a dog picking up fleas. Country dogs are extremely likely to do so. What is disgraceful is neglect of these parasites, which should be dealt with promptly and not allowed to multiply. If they become numerous, it may be necessary to give the dog a medicated bath. Remember, if you are treating your dog for fleas, you must also wash your dog's bedding. These parasites can live in carpets and bedding, and in centrally-heated houses they can be hard to eliminate.

If you live in woody or grazing country, your Whippet may pick up a tick. These parasites hang on to the dog's skin by a mouth-piece, and they become engorged as they suck the dog's blood. Do not attempt to pull the tick off, or you will leave the mouth-piece embedded in the dog's skin, which could result in a nasty infection. The easiest method is to soak the area with an antiseptic, and this will force the tick to release its hold.

Anal glands, which are situated at the root of the tail, may need attention occasionally. If they become too full, they cause discomfort, and will need to be emptied. This is a perfectly simple procedure, and your vet will show you what to do. You must also check that there is no discharge from the anus or from the genital organs, and a constant watch should be kept on bitches for signs of coming in season.

GROOMING

A Whippet requires regular grooming, not only to cleanse the coat, but to stimulate the muscles and the growth of the hair, and also to remove dead hairs. With proper handling and encouragement, your Whippet will soon learn to accept this procedure, and most will look forward to the attention they receive.

Stand your Whippet on a table that is about waist-high in order to avoid backache for the handler, and start off by using a good hound glove, with the little rubber nodules on it. Start at the head and continue over the whole body, brushing vigorously against the lie of the coat in long sweeping movements, with as much weight as possible behind the brush, and continue for as long as possible. This is the massage which tones up the system and does so much good. As your Whippet has a smooth coat, finish off with a chamois leather to give a fine gloss to the coat.

BATHING
When it comes to bath time – and this should not be too often as it destroys the natural oil in the coat – you should use a good brand of special dog shampoo or baby shampoo. Never use a carbolic soap or washing liquid, as they can irritate the skin. A bath or a shower unit is the best place to bath your dog, and you will certainly find it helpful to use a shower spray. Place a non-slip rubber mat for your dog to stand on, and reassure your dog all the time, giving plenty of praise and encouragement. It is essential to keep the water luke-warm throughout the bathing procedure. After you have applied the shampoo, work it up to a rich lather, and you must make sure that all the shampoo is rinsed out of the coat. There are a number of coat conditioners you can apply, and again, you must ensure the coat is thoroughly rinsed. Your Whippet must be towelled dry after bathing, and you can use a hair-dryer (on a low setting) to get the coat completely dry.

TEETH
Your Whippet's teeth must be kept clean, as this will ensure healthy gums and sweet-smelling breath. A good diet, which includes hard biscuits, should help to keep the teeth reasonably clean. However, if tartar collects on the teeth, you will have to clean them. There are many brands of canine toothpaste on the market, and there are also canine toothbrushes available, although these are not necessary, as an ordinary toothbrush will serve just as well.

If your Whippet has a bad accumulation of tartar, you will need to scale the teeth, using a tooth-scaler. This is not a difficult operation, but you would be advised to ask your vet, or an experienced breeder to show you how to do it.

NAILS
The Whippet has well-knuckled feet, rather like the round cat-like feet seen in many other breeds. It is imperative that the feet and nails are kept in good condition, and they should be checked on a regular basis. Pads should be examined to ensure there are no cracks, and you should look between the toes to make sure there are no cysts forming. The nails must be kept short, and regular road-walking will take care of this. However, if the nails are too long they will need to be trimmed on a routine basis.

This can be done with a file, or you can use the guillotine type of nail-cutters. When you cut the nail, you must make sure that you do not cut into the quick, as this will be very painful for the dog, and will result in profuse bleeding. The quick is clearly visible on a white nail, but it is impossible to see on a dark-coloured nail. It is therefore better to be safe rather than sorry, and to cut only the tips off the nails.

WORMING

Whippet puppies invariably carry a roundworm burden, and you should continue the worming programme started by the puppy's breeder. Puppies should be wormed at regular intervals until they are twelve months of age, and then you should worm routinely every six months. This should include a treatment for tapeworms, which can, occasionally, cause problems. The signs of tapeworm infestation are a dull coat, a depraved appetite, and general loss of condition. Fleas form part of the life-cycle of the tapeworm, and so if you keep your dog free from fleas, it will help to eliminate this problem.

EXERCISE

When the dogs are all back in their places, they will settle happily for a while until it is time for a meal. This will be followed by another brief spell outside. Late afternoon is a good time for a walk. Although Whippets can do quite well with very little exercise, they love their outings and will look forward to them.

Whippets have a a marvellous 'internal clock', and most will know exactly when to expect a walk, peering through the window and barking in eager anticipation. If the outing fails to materialise the dog will be terribly disappointed, so you should try to avoid this – even if you can only go out for a few minutes. Whippets have such expressive little faces, to disappoint them is just like disappointing a child. The alteration in them is immediately noticeable – they can change like sunlight into shadow, in a moment. When the brightness is gone, they look downcast and dull.

Whippet puppies begin to enjoy walks at quite an early age and at three or four months they will be racing round the garden. At five months they are ready for their road work, and will quite happily go with the older dogs. By the time they are six months old they will be ready for longer walks, and will be fresh and full of life even if "two legs" are worn out! If you have an enclosed field near at hand, it is lovely to see them fly past in a wild rush, streaming into the field. After fifteen minutes of galloping around, they are ready return to their master, with tongues hanging out and having enjoyed every minute of it.

END OF THE DAY

When the dogs are back in their pens again, it is time to spend a few minutes with any youngsters that are being trained to walk on a lead, or those learning to stand and be handled at shows. Then it will be feeding time again for the puppies, nursing mothers, and for any dogs requiring extra nourishment in order to gain weight and improve condition. The dogs are now coming towards the end of their busy day. Some or all of them will be anxious to join the family for an evening round the fire or watching television. Finally, the dogs will need their last run of the day, followed by another comfortable night snuggled up in cosy beds.

SUMMARY

Whippets thrive as individuals, and they wilt without human companionship and love. They should therefore be included in the family circle whenever possible. This is not always easy if you have a lot of dogs, but you can still allocate time to give individual attention, taking it in turns. For example, you can take one of two dogs out shopping, allow a few dogs to come into your kitchen for a while, or take a couple of dogs out for a drive in the car. Do not aspire to have the biggest kennel: you want the best kennel – and that means every dog receiving the personal care and attention that they so richly deserve.

ADULT NUTRITION

Anyone who contemplates purchasing a Whippet for the first time is usually, and very rightly, much concerned about feeding the correct diet. This is a sensible attitude, because correct diet is the basis of good health, and does much to determine the life-span of any dog. At best, a Whippet's life is far too short, but if you hope to have one for something like thirteen years or so, it is necessary to keep the dog in tip-top condition. In this respect, Whippet owners have no special problems. Indeed, it is probable that the man who buys a Great Dane or similar large breed has a far more complicated task, for nourishing a big animal, providing all the essentials to build a huge frame, complete with compensating strong bones and muscles, is something of an expert's job.

Whippets are not fussy feeders, and the provision of plain, wholesome food is all that is required. In the normal course of events, a Whippet does not require extras such as calcium, cod-liver oil, malt, bran, tonics etc. Many people get the impression that the Whippet is fragile and delicate, although this is far from being so. Whippets that are well cared for and well reared, are every bit as sturdy and strong as any other breed of dog. A Whippet should be fed the same quantity as any other dog of similar size. Naturally, the flesh foods should be chopped or minced, and the biscuit meal should be of the terrier size, with the finely ground biscuit for puppies.

Beware of leaving tempting food unattended when your Whippet is about. Far from being a fool, your Whippet is as smart as paint. If you leave food on the table and it smells tasty, all you have to do is turn your back, and your dog will display astonishing speed and skill in the art of stealing. There is no doubt that the Whippet is the best thief in the canine race!

FLESH DIETS

Whippets do best on a diet consisting mainly of meat, which can be fed raw or lightly cooked. Meat is a natural food and nourishes without producing over-rapid growth or coarse, spongy bone. Is any kind of meat suitable? This is the question I am most commonly asked when people come to buy a puppy. I recommend feeding lean beef, mutton or breast of lamb. Pork should never be fed: it is too rich for dogs and is inclined to upset their digestion. It is to be avoided at all costs.

Feeding too much biscuit distends the stomach without providing salt, minerals and vitamins necessary to canine health. Boiled tripe is relished, but the bleached tripe sold by the butcher is not popular with dogs, and the preparation used to whiten it is thought to be harmful, possibly causing stomach troubles. Fish should always be boiled, and it must be carefully boned. The danger of small bones or splinters of bone cannot be too strongly emphasised. They are exceedingly dangerous: you must ensure they are never fed to a dog, or discarded where a dog might find them.

CANNED FOOD

Canned meat, produced specially for dogs, is sold in great quantities and there are many different brands to choose from. Some brands seem better than others, particularly those containing tightly-packed lean meat, without a lot of watery, jelly substances. Avoid the type which contains cereals and other things; dogs seem to eat this only if there is nothing more appetising on offer. Canned food is a highly convenient method of feeding your dog, particularly if you are travelling or at show. It is always useful to keep a few cans for an emergency, but nothing can really take the place of fresh meat. It is the natural food for the carnivore, regardless of how the manufacturers try to persuade us that their canned products are in every way its equal. It is unlikely that your dog will suffer any harm if fed exclusively on canned food, but it is hard to believe that the valuable mineral salts, vitamins and other nutrients are found in a heat-treated product. Nothing can be better than fresh, natural food. Canned meat may be easier to obtain and pleasanter to handle, but although it is certainly a useful standby for occasional use, it is not recommended as a staple diet.

BISCUITS

There are many makes of biscuits, and the famous name and the high price are not necessarily a guarantee of superior quality. Dogs undoubtedly show decided preferences for certain kinds of biscuits. Once they take a fancy to a make and get it regularly, they do not seem to appreciate a change. They prefer to have the same brand, especially if it is mixed with something different from time to time. The meat can be served cooked one day, raw the next, or a little fish stirred in.

Use your judgment when selecting a biscuit meal. If it is clean, wholemeal, free from dust, sweet-smelling, and without a trace of mustiness, it is probably a good meal irrespective of price. Whitemeal should be avoided, and this also applies to white bread. Do not be dazzled by meals made up of confetti-like fragments. The colours often mean nothing at all; they have no particular flavours, and are put in "because the owners like them". They have no advantage over the plain meal. Brown wholemeal biscuits are the wisest choice; avoid the 'pin-head' type that goes pasty when soaked – most dogs dislike this intensely.

Young Whippets enjoy the small oval-shaped biscuits sold by leading dog-food manufacturers. These are sometimes coloured and do vary in flavour, but most dogs find them attractive. Older dogs should also be given these biscuits. It is surprising how the 'oldies' in the kennel, many of them with one or two teeth missing, manage to eat these hard-baked biscuits and will never be left out when they are on offer.

VEGETABLES

Opinions are divided on the question of giving dogs vegetables. Veterinary authorities tell us that raw vegetables have to be very finely chopped for the dog to derive any benefits from them at all, otherwise they pass out of the system without being utilized by the digestive organs. One school of thought believes that cooked vegetables are of very little value to the dog. A few carrots and onions boiled up with the meat and stock certainly help to make it tasty, and a sprinkling of finely-chopped, uncooked parsley or grated raw carrot may well be beneficial, although dogs seem to get on very well without these things. Potatoes should not be given in quantity, and if a little is fed from time to time, it must be well-mashed.

COMPLETE DIETS
Some of the top breeders feed complete diets to their dogs, and their dogs seem to do well on it. However, I still advocate the traditional method of feeding as being the most natural for a dog. There are many different types of complete diet, and again, these vary in quality. If you do feed a complete diet, it is essential to go for a top-quality brand. Remember that these diets are specially formulated to provide a complete and balanced diet, and so you should not add any supplements. There are different diets provided for particular needs, such as lactating bitches, working dogs, or veterans, and so you can provide the diet to suit your dog's individual requirements.

FLUIDS
Fresh water must be available at all times, particularly if you are feeding a complete diet. Many half-grown and adult Whippets are very partial to a drink of milk and will prefer it to water. Milk is also a useful conditioner, and of particular value for a show dog requiring a little extra weight and bloom. Sometimes a sweetened rice pudding or custard is popular.

QUANTITY
How much food should a Whippet receive? This is not an easy question to answer because requirements vary with each dog. A Whippet is a fair eater for its size, but, of course, the amount consumed is small compared with the quantity larger dogs will eat. If you are a bit concerned about your Whippet's weight, the best guide is appearance. If your dog polishes the dish clean, yet still looks much the same shape, you probably need to feed a little more food. If on the other hand, your dog has finished eating and looks blown out, distended and uncomfortable, you are clearly feeding too much, and only two-thirds of that quantity should be offered the following day. The good keeper of livestock is very quick to observe such signs as these. It is far better to be guided by physical appearance than to collect diet sheets and books, attempting to be guided by the written word alone. This policy of observation has long-term benefits in that you can adjust the diet according to the individual's requirements. If your Whippet looks lean, you will need to offer more food, and possibly tempt the dog's appetite with something particularly tasty. If your Whippet is putting on excess weight, the allowance must be scaled down. The aim is to have a dog that is eating the same quantity every day, maintaining weight, and looking in top-class condition – firm and well-covered, but neither skinny nor fat.

MAINTAINING CONDITION
There can be few experienced dog show exhibitors who have not suffered the maddening defeats in the ring caused – according to the subsequent critiques from the judges – by the fact that an exhibit was either too fat or too thin. It is easier to solve the problem of an overweight dog. All that is needed is to feed a diet consisting entirely of meat, reduced in quantity, with all tidbits eliminated. This, along with plenty of exercise, will put matters right in a short time.

A well-cared for Whippet is neither too fat nor too thin, with a sleek shining coat, and bright, sparkling eyes.
Carol Anne Johnson.

It is more difficult to put weight on a dog. Young dogs, in particular, can be tiresome about food. They are upset by all sorts of things: the proximity of bitches in season, travelling, strange surroundings, changes in their menu, even by sounds such as footsteps, doors being opened and closed, traffic, and so on. Whatever the cause, the poor feeder will look at the carefully prepared bowl of food, give it a casual sniff or a look of disgust, and walk away. The accepted procedure is to take the food away, and to wait until the next day before offering food again, and repeat this procedure until hunger forces its acceptance. This sounds fine in theory, but in practice, at least where a show dog is concerned, it is hopeless. While the 'cure' is in progress, the dog is getting thinner and thinner. If the dog does eat, you may well find that with appetite satisfied, you are back to the routine of the dog refusing meals again, until hunger pangs become really acute. This is no way to condition a dog. It may be alright for a pet, if the owner is not temporarily concerned about appearance, but the owner of a show dog requires peak condition in order to be successful in the ring.

To most people, the sight of a thin and poor-looking dog is depressing and worrying. If the dog is to gain weight, you must coax and encourage until you have a return of appetite. There are various ways of doing this. One well-known breeder friend would bake some Yorkshire puddings, and leave them on the table so that the dog she was showing would steal them. The dog thought that he had got one over on her, but all the time she was laughing up her sleeve! It certainly solved the problem, because in no time he had gained the weight that he needed. There are other methods that can be tried. Mixing the ordinary rations with either grated cheese or malt bread often has a magical result. Meat, grilled with a spot of butter, is hard to resist. Chicken, or chopped, baked liver generally tempt the most capricious appetite. Some picky feeders will eat quite a lot of food if it is handed to them, piece by piece, from the table, yet will ignore it if it is put on the floor in a dog dish. There are even some crafty characters who will eat when they think they are stealing the cat's food, yet refuse the same food when it is fed to them. If there is something that the dog really likes, go ahead and provide it. Do not waste time trying to persuade your dog to eat other foods which you may feel would be more beneficial. It is far better for a dog to eat up and enjoy the food, than for you to watch your dog daily losing condition because of lack of interest in the food you are providing.

It is beneficial to show dogs if they will take a milk-and-cereal breakfast, and still eat a substantial main meal later in the day. If, however, the sloppy meal spoils the appetite for the meat etc., it is best to drop it and to concentrate on persuading the dog to enjoy a good solid feed. The same thing applies to the 'extras' people give to their dogs when they are trying to get them into better condition. There are all kinds of useful supplements – yeast tablets, seaweed powder, vitamin powders and tablets, cod-liver oil, compound tonics containing iron and minerals, condition powders, and so on – the dog papers are packed with advertisements for them, the trade stands at dog shows are loaded with them, and chemists and herbalists also stock them. Some are invaluable, most are useful, but few are palatable, the exception being the yeast capsules which most dogs eat with relish.

If the dog does not care for the taste of a powder or liquid, it is foolish to sprinkle it on food, which is certain to be rejected. The food alone, if eaten, would have done the dog some good. If it is refused, the tonic preparation actually does harm, since it revolts the dog and a nourishing meal is refused. Only a greedy dog, the proverbial 'good-doer', will gobble up a dish of food mixed with a strong-tasting medicine or powder. If you decide that a member of the kennel requires a tonic, it is best to choose a tasteless variety, otherwise you defeat your object. Offer fresh, good, nourishing food, and do all you can to persuade the dog to eat it. This is the best way of providing a dog with the essentials that will help to achieve, and maintain, top show condition.

TRAINING YOUR WHIPPET

The Whippet is easy to teach because it is amazingly intelligent. This breed is living proof that dogs *can* reason. Given the sketchiest knowledge of dog psychology, it is perfectly possible to watch a Whippet working out a problem when in full flight. There are no dull or stupid Whippets, but there are, occasionally, some owners who lack the ability to transmit to their dogs the things they would like them to do. In this instance, the fault lies with the owners, not with their animals.

COLLAR AND LEAD TRAINING

While the house-training is in progress, it is a good idea to accustom the puppy to a collar and a lead. Walks will probably not begin for some time, as you cannot take your puppy out until the inoculation programme has been completed, but it is much better to introduce new experiences gradually. Choose a very fine, light collar, preferably one made of soft leather. Make sure that it fits properly: it must not be tight – you should be able to slip a couple of fingers inside the collar when it is fastened round your puppy's neck. Equally, it must not be loose enough to slip past the ears. Some puppies scratch at a new collar, and you must ensure that there is no risk of a paw getting caught up inside the collar, leading to an injury.

I suggest that you first try putting the collar on your puppy just before feeding time. Instead of disliking the feeling of constraint, the puppy will associate the collar with a pleasant occurrence. All attention will be focused on the arrival of the food dish, and your puppy will be far less likely to scratch or rub the collar in an attempt to remove it.

As soon as your puppy is used to the collar, you can try attaching a light lead. Let this trail about after the dog for a bit, then pick up the loop and try to attract the puppy towards you, using a tidbit and encouraging words as an incentive. Always give plenty of praise when your puppy reaches you, even though the pup may have been slow to respond. Never be cross when your Whippet is close to you. In the puppy's mind it is important to make the connection that disagreeable things only happen when you are some distance away. Coming to you, and reaching you, must be regarded as something enjoyable. The puppy must feel confident that your hands mean stroking and loving, so there is always a motive for coming back to you. This is the best way to own an obedient dog – one that comes running to you the moment you call.

When you start lead-training, the puppy will move away and then may panic and struggle as the lead tightens. It is difficult for the puppy to understand where the constraint is coming from. In this instance, stand firm, call your dog to you by name, and coax gently until you draw your puppy towards you. As soon as your Whippet is within reach, reward with plenty

Barmoll Beaujolais at Teisanlap. If you start teaching from an early age, your Whippet will soon learn to accept the collar and lead.

of praise and petting. If the puppy comes to you willingly, make an extra special fuss, and reward with a game, a tidbit, and lots of love. Make sure the tidbit you provide is something really tasty – a scrap of cheese, or a bit of chicken – so the Whippet really looks forward to the training treats. In the early stages, reward your puppy, even if progress is slow. As soon as your Whippet understands what is required, you will be surprised at how quickly you progress. Do not make training sessions long and arduous. A puppy does not have the concentration, and you will make the experience something to be dreaded rather than something to enjoy. Training should be fun, and five minutes or so, night and day, are quite sufficient for a youngster. If regularly adhered to, this routine is much more successful than a longer period once or twice a week. It is surprising how soon there is some progress, and how jauntily the puppy will be trotting beside you.

TRAVELLING WITH YOUR WHIPPET
A puppy should be accustomed to going about in a vehicle fairly early in life, as soon as the inoculation programme has been completed. When your Whippet is behaving well on the lead, you are ready to attempt short journeys. If you are travelling by car, it is advisable to accommodate your dog in a crate, or at least in a safe area of the car. To begin with, your puppy may be upset, or possibly car-sick – Whippets are notoriously bad travellers – so make sure you take a towel and some paper towels with you in case of an emergency!

It is a good idea to get your Whippet used to the car gradually. Allow your dog to sit in the car when it is stationary, and then go on short journeys, ending up with a walk or a game, so that your dog associates the car with something pleasurable. You may find it helpful to have a passenger who can concentrate on reassuring the dog while you drive. If car-sickness continues to be a problem, you vet may suggest trying some travel-sickness tablets.

TRAINING TARGETS
If your Whippet is destined to be your best friend, but nothing more, you may be content with this amount of basic Obedience. However, if you are hoping to show your Whippet, there is much more to learn, all of which is very important.

Chapter Four

THE BREED STANDARD

Every breed of pedigree dog has a Breed Standard that is approved by the national Kennel Club, and must be adhered to by every judge who judges in that country. The American Standard describes the Whippet in greater depth than the British Standard, which follows a truncated format that has been drawn up for all Breed Standards. The American Standard lists more faults which should be penalised than the British equivalent, and it also has a number of disqualifications. However, the two main differences between the Standards relate to size and pigmentation. The Federation Cynologique Internationale is based in Belgium and it governs the activities of pedigree dogs in Europe, including Scandinavia, plus South America, Mexico and Japan. The FCI takes the Standard from a breed's country of origin, and in the case of the Whippet it follows the British Standard, with one exception, and that is in relation to size.

BRITISH BREED STANDARD

GENERAL APPEARANCE
Balanced combination of muscular power and strength with elegance and grace of outline. Built for speed and work. All forms of exaggeration should be avoided.

CHARACTERISTICS
An ideal companion. Highly adaptable in domestic and sporting surroundings.

TEMPERAMENT
Gentle, affectionate, even disposition.

HEAD AND SKULL
Long and lean, flat on top tapering to muzzle with slight stop, rather wide between the eyes, jaws powerful and clean-cut, nose black, in blues a bluish colour permitted, in livers a nose of the same colour, in whites or parti-colour a butterfly nose permissible.

EYES
Oval, bright, expression very alert.

POINTS OF ANATOMY

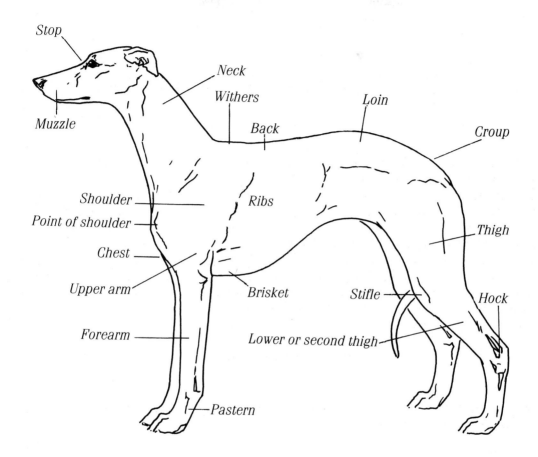

EARS
Rose-shaped, small, fine in texture.

MOUTH
Jaws strong with a perfect, regular and complete scissor bite, i.e. upper teeth closely overlapping lower teeth and set square to the jaws.

NECK
Long, muscular, elegantly arched.

GOOD CONFORMATION

Illustrated by Ch. Dyanne Dondelayo.   *Diane Pearce.*

FOREQUARTERS
Shoulders oblique and muscular, blades carried up to top of spine, where they are clearly defined. Forelegs straight and upright, front not too wide, pasterns strong with slight spring, elbows set well under body.

BODY
Chest very deep with plenty of heart room, brisket deep, well defined, broad back, firm, somewhat long, showing definite arch over loin but not humped. Loin giving impression of strength and power, ribs well sprung, muscled on back.

HINDQUARTERS
Strong, broad across thighs, stifles well bent, hocks well let down, well developed second thighs, dog able to stand over a lot of ground and show great driving power.

FEET
Very neat, well split up between toes, knuckles well arched, pads thick and strong.

TAIL
No feathering. Long, tapering, when in action carried in a delicate curve upward but not over back.

GAIT/MOVEMENT
Free, hindlegs coming well under body for propulsion. Forelegs thrown well forward low over the ground, true coming and going. General movement not to look stilted, high stepping, short or mincing.

COAT
Fine, short, close in texture.

COLOUR
Any colour or mixture of colours.

SIZE
Height: dogs: 47-51 cms (18½-20 ins); bitches: 44-47 cms (17-18½ ins).

FAULTS
Any departure from the foregoing points should be considered a fault and the seriousness with which the fault should be regarded should be in exact proportion to its degree.

NOTE: Male animals should have two apparently normal testicles fully descended into the scrotum.

Reproduced by kind permission of the English Kennel Club.

AMERICAN BREED STANDARD

GENERAL APPEARANCE
A medium size sighthound giving the appearance of elegance and fitness denoting great speed, power and balance without coarseness. A true sporting hound that covers a maximum of distance with a minimum of lost motion. Should convey an impression of beautifully balanced muscular power and strength, combined with great elegance and grace of outline. Symmetry of outline, muscular development and powerful gait are the main considerations; the dog being built for speed and work, all forms of exaggeration should be avoided.

SIZE, PROPORTION, SUBSTANCE

Ideal height for dogs, 19 to 22 inches, for bitches, 18 to 21 inches, measured at the highest point of the withers. One-half inch above or below the stated limits will disqualify. Length from forechest to buttocks equal to or slightly greater than height at the withers. Moderate bone throughout.

HEAD

Keen intelligent alert expression. *Eyes* large and dark. Both eyes must be of the same color. Yellow or light eyes should be strictly penalized. Blue or wall eyes shall disqualify. Fully pigmented eyelids are desirable.

Rose *ears,* small, fine in texture; in repose, thrown back and folded along neck. Fold should be maintained when at attention. Erect ears should be severely penalized.

Skull long and lean, fairly wide between the ears, scarcely perceptible stop. *Muzzle* should be long and powerful, denoting great strength of bite, without coarseness. Lack of underjaw should be strictly penalized. *Nose* entirely black. *Teeth* of upper jaw should fit closely over teeth of lower jaw creating a scissors bite. Teeth should be white and strong. Undershot shall disqualify. Overshot one-quarter inch or more shall disqualify.

NECK, TOPLINE, BODY

Neck long, clean and muscular, well arched with no suggestion of throatiness, widening gracefully into the top of the shoulder. A short thick neck, or a ewe neck, should be penalized.

The *back* is broad, firm and well muscled, having length over the loin. The backline runs smoothly from the withers with a graceful natural arch, not too accentuated, beginning over the loin and carrying through over the croup; the arch is continuous without flatness. A dip behind shoulder blades, wheelback, flat back, or a steep or flat croup should be penalized.

Brisket very deep, reaching as nearly as possible to the point of the elbow. *Ribs* well sprung but with no suggestion of barrel shape. The space between the forelegs is filled in so that there is no appearance of a hollow between them. There is a definite tuck-up of the underline.

The *tail* long and tapering, reaching to the hipbone when drawn through between the hind legs. When the dog is in motion, the tail is carried low with only a gentle upward curve; tail should not be carried higher than top of back.

FOREQUARTERS

Shoulder blade long, well laid back, with flat muscles, allowing for moderate space between shoulder blades at peak of withers. Upper arm of equal length, placed so that the elbow falls directly under the withers. The points of the elbows should point neither in nor out, but straight back. A steep shoulder, short upper arm, a heavily muscled or loaded shoulder, or a very narrow shoulder, all of which restrict low free movement, should be strictly penalized. *Forelegs* straight, giving appearance of strength of bone. Pasterns strong, slightly bent and flexible. Bowed legs, tied-in elbows, legs lacking substance, legs set far under the body so as to create an exaggerated forechest, weak or upright pasterns should be strictly penalized. Both front and rear feet must be well formed with hard, thick pads. Feet more hare than cat, but both are acceptable. Flat, splayed or soft feet without thick hard pads should be strictly penalized. Toes should be long, close and well arched. Nails strong and naturally short or of moderate length. Dewclaws may be removed.

HINDQUARTERS
Long and powerful. The thighs are broad and muscular, stifles well bent; muscles are long and flat and carry well down toward the hock. The hocks are well let down and close to the ground. Sickle or cow hocks should be strictly penalized.

COAT
Short, close, smooth and firm in texture. Any other coat shall be a disqualification. Old scars and injuries, the result of work or accident, should not be allowed to prejudice the dog's chance in the show ring.

COLOR
Color immaterial.

GAIT
Low, free moving and smooth, with reach in the forequarters and strong drive in the hindquarters. The dog has great freedom of action when viewed from the side; the forelegs move forward close to the ground to give a long low reach; the hindlegs have strong propelling power. When moving and viewed from front or rear, legs should turn neither in nor out, nor should feet cross or interfere with each other.

   Lack of front reach or rear drive, or a short hackney gait with high wrist action, should be strictly penalized. Crossing in front or moving too close should be strictly penalized.

TEMPERAMENT
Amiable, friendly, gentle, but capable of great intensity during sporting pursuits.

DISQUALIFICATIONS
One-half inch above or below stated height limits.
Blue or wall eyes.
Undershot, overshot one-quarter inch or more.
Any coat other than short, close, smooth and firm in texture.

Reproduced by kind permission of the American Kennel Club.
Approved December 11, 1989.   *Effective February 1, 1990.*

ANALYSIS AND INTERPRETATION

GENERAL APPEARANCE

The Breed Standard calls for a balanced combination of muscular power and strength, with elegance and grace of outline. This breed is built for speed and work, and all forms of exaggeration should be avoided. A Whippet's outline should flow from the tip of the nose to the end of the tail. The dog should stand over the ground naturally with a stance which should not appear cramped in any way.

A top-class Whippet should always have the look of a thoroughbred. It can never achieve this if shown in a fat and flabby condition. The perfect muscle tone required for a Whippet does not mean ugly, bulging muscles. The muscle should be hard and flat.

Ch. Nutshell of Nevedith: British breed record holder with forty-seven CCs, and Reserve Best in Show, Crufts 1990.
Bred by Mr and Mrs Barker, owned by Miss E. Newton.

The Whippet should look like a thoroughbred – a balanced combination of muscular power and strength, coupled with elegance and grace of outline.

THE BODY

The desired grace of outline can only be achieved by the length and strength of the neck, which is also a prerequisite for a hunting dog that needs to pick up prey. The correct neck can only be achieved if a dog has the correct lay of shoulder. If a Whippet is straight in shoulder and short in upper arm, the neck will look stuffy, as though it is just stuck on top of

THE BODY

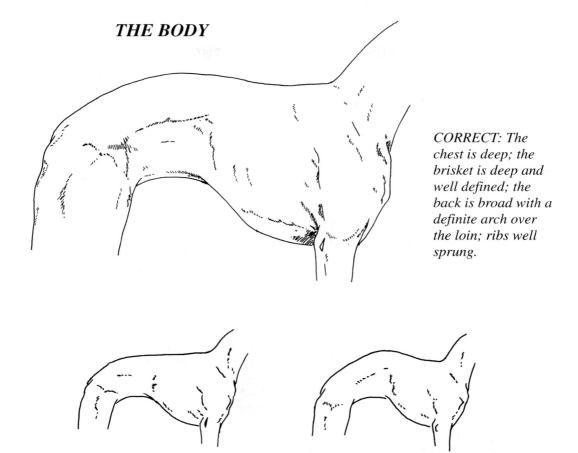

CORRECT: The chest is deep; the brisket is deep and well defined; the back is broad with a definite arch over the loin; ribs well sprung.

INCORRECT: The topline is too flat.

INCORRECT: Roached or wheel-back.

the body. Such a dog will never move with the desired long and low reach stride. It will move more like a hackney pony, which is highly undesirable.

The brisket should be deep and ribs well-sprung. Barrel ribs are incorrect. This is the area that accommodates the heart, and there must be sufficient space, combined with the correct width of the chest. The back should be strong and fairly long, with a definite arch over the loin, which the dog should retain on the move. A roach or wheel-back is a very serious fault. A dog which has this usually has incorrect shoulder placement and straight stifles. The flat back is also very undesirable and shows a form of weakness over the loin.

I prefer the wording on the topline of the American Standard: "The back is broad and firm and well muscled, having length over the loin. The backline runs smoothly from the withers with a graceful natural arch, not too accentuated; beginning over the loin and carrying through to the croup, the arch is continuous without flatness. A dip behind shoulder blades,

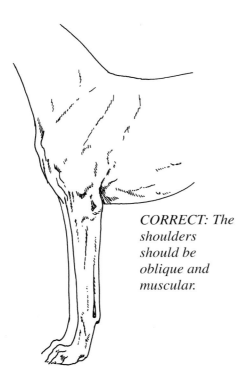

FOREQUARTERS

CORRECT: The shoulders should be oblique and muscular.

The forelegs should be straight, and the front not too wide.

Shalfleet Sequality of Walkabout: This Whippet shows the correct fill between the front legs.

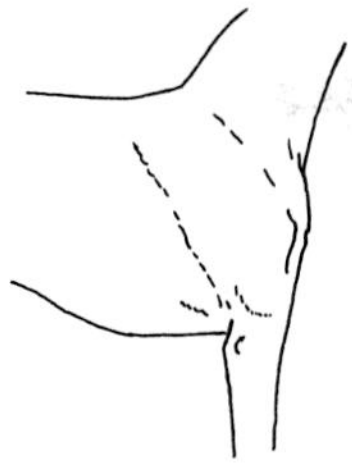

INCORRECT:
Straight or
short upper
arm.

INCORRECT:
No depth of
chest.

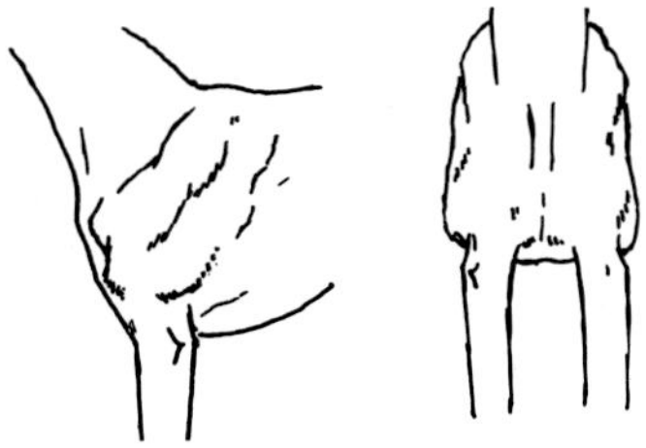

INCORRECT: Loaded shoulders.

INCORRECT:
Too narrow.

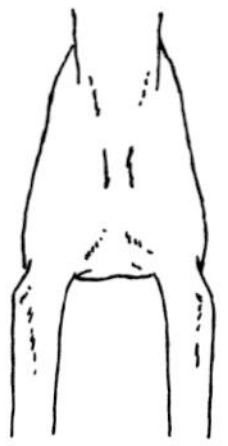

INCORRECT:
Too wide, out
at elbow.

INCORRECT:
Toeing in.

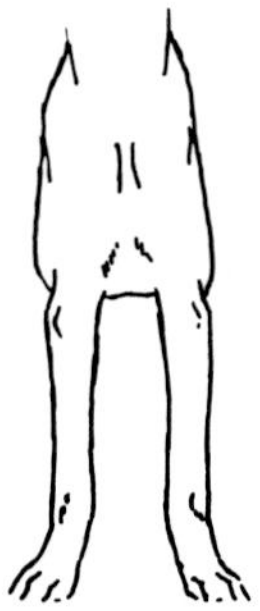

INCORRECT:
Toes at '10 to 2'.

wheel-back, flat back, or a croup that is steep or flat should be penalised." I think this gives a clearer picture of the topline.

The stifle should be well bent with a strong second thigh and short hock, enabling the hind legs to be brought well under the body so that the Whippet can move with the desired drive and length of stride.

HINDQUARTERS

*Broad across the the thighs, stifles well bent, hocks
well let down, and well-developed second thighs.*

CORRECT.   *CORRECT.*

*INCORRECT:
Straight stifle.*

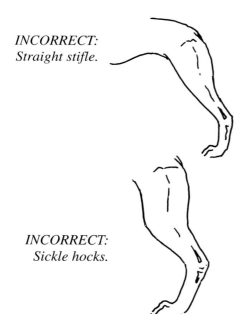

*INCORRECT:
Over-
angulation.*

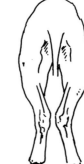

*INCORRECT:
Sickle hocks.*

*INCORRECT:
Cow hocks.*

FEET

The feet must be strong, compact, and tight, but it must be remembered that the Whippet is a running dog, so the foot should not be too bunched. The foot should never be either flat or loose. The Whippet should never be straight in pastern; the spring of pastern acts as a shock-absorber and is vitally important in all running dogs.

FEET

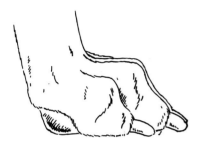

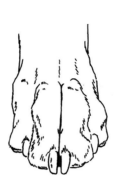

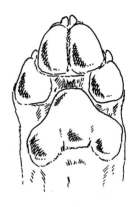

CORRECT: The knuckles should be well arched.

CORRECT: The feet should be very neat, and well split up between the toes.

CORRECT: The pads should be thick and strong.

TAIL

The tail acts as a rudder, so the length is important. It should be tapering with no feather. When in action, the tail is carried with a delicate upward curve. It should never be carried over the back.

TAIL

CORRECT: The tail should be long and tapering, and carried in a delicate upward curve when in action.

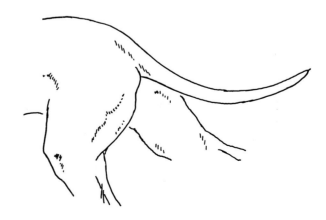

HEAD

The old Whippet breeders used to say that a good Whippet started behind the collar. This is true to some extent, and certainly the structure of the head would not be so important in a working dog, but in a show Whippet the head does add the finishing touch. A dog should always look masculine and a bitch feminine. Personally, I would prefer a slightly doggy bitch to a feminine dog.

HEAD AND SKULL

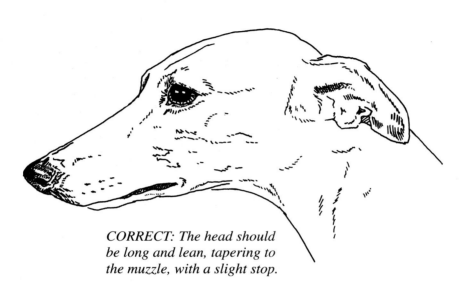

CORRECT: The head should be long and lean, tapering to the muzzle, with a slight stop.

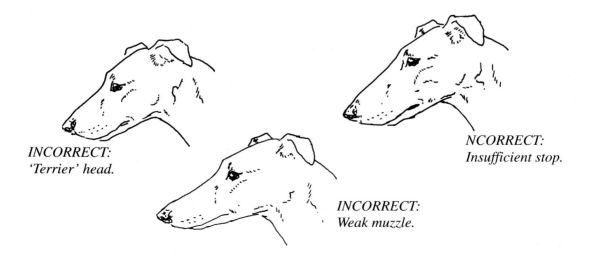

INCORRECT: 'Terrier' head.

INCORRECT: Weak muzzle.

NCORRECT: Insufficient stop.

Ch. Walkabout Warrior King showing a keen and alert expression.

Diane Pearce.

THE NECK

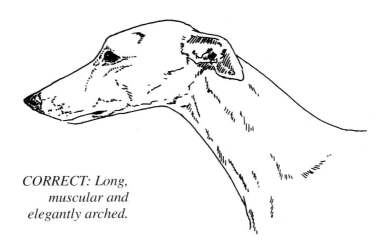

CORRECT: Long, muscular and elegantly arched.

INCORRECT NECKS

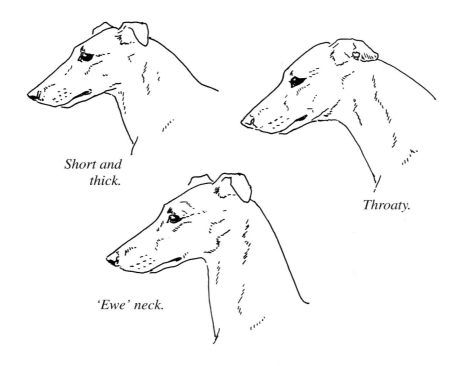

*Short and
thick.*

Throaty.

'Ewe' neck.

EYES

The eyes should be bright, alert and oval in shape. In the British Standard it states that the eye-colour should match the coat. I personally prefer a dark eye, but obviously you have to judge to the Standard. The American Standard differs, asking for the eyes to be large and dark, and yellow or light eyes are strictly penalised.

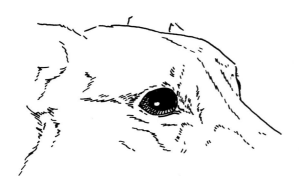

EYES

*CORRECT: The eyes
should be oval, bright,
with an alert expression.*

EARS

The ears should be rose-shaped and fine in texture. They should not be pricked, and happily this seems to be less of a problem that it was a few years ago. The British and American Standards agree on the shape of the ear, but the American Standard severely penalises a prick ear.

EARS

CORRECT: The ears should be rose-shaped and fine in texture.

MOUTH

The mouth calls for a regular and complete scissor bite, upper teeth closely overlapping the lower teeth and set square to the jaw. An overshot bite tends to be evident in dogs with a weak underjaw. At the moment there are too many Whippets with weak underjaws, and if weak underjaws become prevalent, so will the overshot bite.

MOUTH

CORRECT: The jaws must meet in a perfect, regular and complete scissor bite.

CORRECT: The upper teeth must closely overlap the lower teeth.

INCORRECT BITES

Overshot.   *Undershot.*   *Level bite.*

PIGMENT
The British Standard allows for a bluish nose to be permitted in blue-coloured dogs, and a liver nose of the same colour in liver-coloured Whippets. In fact, I have never seen a real liver-coloured Whippet. I find that this colour nose usually goes with the very pale cream fawns. In white and parti-colours a butterfly nose is permissible. The American Standard requires fully pigmented eyelids, and the nose must be entirely black.

COAT AND COLOUR
The Whippet should have a fine coat and skin, and this is so important in the quality look of the breed. They can be any colour or mixture of colours.

MOVEMENT

Nimrodel Peerless showing good forward reach and ground-covering ability.

E. Walsh

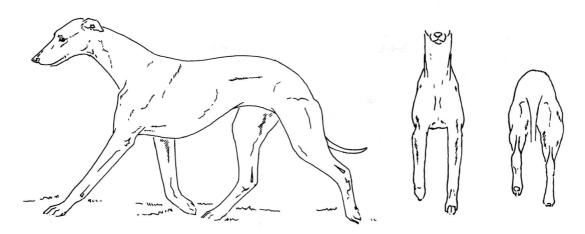

CORRECT: Movement should be free, never looking stilted.

CORRECT: Forelegs should be thrown well forward. Hindlegs should come well under the body for propulsion.

Line drawings by Vivienne Rainsbury, courtesy of the Whippet Breed Council.

SIZE

Size has been an age-old problem in the breed. It is the principal difference between the American and the British Whippet, and it is the only point of difference between the British and the FCI Standards. The British Standard stipulates: Dogs 47 to 51 cms (18½ to 20 ins) and bitches 44 to 47 cms (17½ to 18½ ins). The American Standard requires a much bigger dog, with the ideal height for dogs at 19 to 22 inches, and 18 to 21 inches for bitches, measured at the highest point of the withers. One-half inch above or below the stated limits will disqualify a dog from the American show ring. The FCI Standard comes midway between these two extremes, asking for dogs to be a maximum height of 51 cms (20½ ins), and bitches to be 48 cms (just under 19½ ins).

Although the British Standard asks for a much smaller Whippet, it is true to say that there have not been any really top-class animals at the smaller end of the scale, i.e. an 18½ ins dog or a 17½ ins bitch. Personally, I would not show a dog over 20½ inches, or a bitch over 19 inches. I believe that if a Whippet gets too big and coarse, you stand the risk of losing type, which is the most important thing of all. The British Standard has no disqualification clauses and the decision is left to the discretion of the judge.

Despite this significant difference in size regulations, many British Champions have gained their titles in America, and I am sure that many Champion Whippets in America could gain their titles in the UK.

Chapter Five

THE SHOW SCENE

The Whippet is one of the easiest breeds to prepare for the show ring, and you must ensure your dog is always presented in pristine condition. This is a breed that is very eager to please, quick to learn, and does not require any rough treatment. I deplore rough-handling in the ring, be it by a judge or by an exhibitor. If your Whippet will not show or refuses to move when you get into the ring, you have only yourself to blame!

SHOW TRAINING

Every breeder has their own ideas about what age to start show training. Personally, I do not think you can start too young. By eight weeks my puppies are usually very confident at being stood on a table. However, it is important to make sure the table is very steady, and not slippery. I put a car mat on the table, and I find this provides the ideal surface. At this stage it does not matter if the puppy does not stand perfectly still. The aim is to build up the puppy's confidence, and to make sure your puppy enjoys these mini training sessions.

While the puppy is on the table, I check teeth and ears, but I never do anything to the nails – attempting to do this would be a sure way to frighten the puppy from ever wanting to go on to a table again. When I want to attend to nails, I sit with the puppy on my lap. The puppy is encouraged to lie with tummy upwards, and I gently hold the foot and take the tip off each nail with a file. I never cut the nails. The nails should be filed once a week, as no amount of walking seems to keep a Whippet's nails in trim.

I start lead training when a puppy is about twelve weeks of age. I use a nylon show slip-lead, but not one with a ring on the end, which acts as a choke. At this age your puppy will not have had its full course of inoculations, so you will not be able to leave your own premises. Training will therefore take place in the house and garden. I slip the lead round the puppy's neck and then give the puppy a tidbit. I always move with the puppy, and never drag the puppy to come with me. This is done for about five minutes a day. Once the puppy associates having the lead slipped on with receiving a tidbit, there will be no problem about the pup following you.

By four months of age, the puppy will be ready for the outside world. I usually take the puppy's dam on the first outing as well, but if this is your first Whippet, you will not have this option. For the first outing, I never take the puppy more than fifty yards up the road. When a car appears, I stop and bend down to stroke and reassure the puppy. If you give

The fruits of success: Ch. Pencloe Dutch Gold, pictured winning Best in Show Crufts 1992, with owner-breeder Morag Bolton.

plenty of encouragement, the puppy will very quickly get used to the noise and traffic. After a few days, the puppy will look forward to the daily outing every day, and you can now start some serious training. Most local canine societies have ring training classes, some with monthly match meetings. These are very enjoyable social events and are very much looked forward to. It is a place to make friends in your own breed, as well as breed enthusiasts. However, do not be tempted to drag your puppy there week after week. Give the puppy a rest, and just attend by yourself. You can still be learning by watching other handlers.

RING PRESENCE

By building your Whippet's confidence slowly over the months, you will find that when you enter the show ring for the first time, your dog will be familiar with the handling stance and movements required, and will therefore appear bright, alert, and confident. A dog's presence or showmanship is a crucial feature in show judging. This presence has a lot to do with good handling.

If you are not sufficiently confident yourself, this will transfer to the dog. Dogs pick up human moods, and this is especially true of Whippets. A gloomy owner will soon transmit their feeling to the dog, and the result will be a drab and lacklustre performance. Remember that even though the judge is looking at your dog, you should dress smartly, preferably in a colour to complement your dog. Footwear should be practical and comfortable.

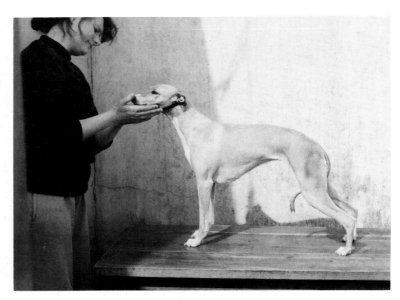

Whippets are taught to stand on a table for the judge's inspection.

MOVING YOUR WHIPPET

One of the most important aspects of your performance in the show ring is the way your Whippet moves. The judge will require you to move your Whippet at a brisk walk, first round the ring with the others in the class, then each dog is examined on the table. Most judges will indicate a triangle for individual movement, giving a chance to assess the dog's action from the rear, from the side, and then coming towards the judge. When moving, a Whippet should never be strung up on a tight lead. A dog cannot move freely if you do this.

If you are new to showing, do not be the first to be seen. Go to the end of the line, and watch the other handlers carefully. After the triangle, the judge often asks dog and handler to move straight up and down. Listen carefully to the judge, and try to do everything you are told. Good judges are always sympathetic to the new and nervous exhibitor.

POSING YOUR WHIPPET

When standing, good handlers accomplish a show pose with a minimum of fuss. I find the best technique for standing a Whippet is to place one hand under the brisket, and raise the front end, allowing it to drop into place. Arrange the hindlegs with the hocks parallel to the ground. If you over-stretch a Whippet you will straighten the stifle and the topline will cut away. A Whippet should cover the ground naturally, and if stood correctly your dog will feel comfortable and will not fidget. Do not make your dog stand for too long. When the judge is not looking in your direction, allow your dog to relax and give plenty of praise – but keep your eye on the judge at all times.

PRESENTATION

We are very lucky with the Whippet being one of the easier breeds to prepare for the show ring. The only trimming they require is under the tail. If you are not confident enough to do

Nevedith Justa Jenie learning to move on the lead, expertly handled by Nev Newton. A Whippet must be given the opportunity to move freely – this breed should never be 'strung up' when on the move.

At five months, Nevedith Justa Jenie has already learned to pose, showing herself off to advantage.

In the show ring, the handler must keep calm and relaxed so that nerves do not travel down the lead to affect the dog's confidence.

The Whippet is an easy dog to prepare for the show ring. The hardest task is maintaining your dog at top quality. Ch. Welstar Royal Mint looks in perfect condition at eight years of age.

this, or you are not sure how much hair to take off, leave it, and ask one of the exhibitors when you get to the show. They will be only too pleased to show you. I find once the tail has been trimmed expertly, you will only have to tidy the stray hairs about once a month.

Grooming should be carried out every day. This is not a chore – Whippets love it! I use a rubber pad to take away loose hairs, followed by a thorough brushing, and a good massage with the hands. I finish off with a polish, using a piece of silk, velvet or a chamois leather. You will find that solid fawns do not really require bathing specially for a show, but if they have white trim I always wash that part the night before. I always bath parti-colours two nights before a show. I use a baby shampoo, which is mild and will not sting the eyes. In Britain, the Kennel Club do not allow the use of chalk or powders that stay in the coat while a dog is being judged. However, you can use them for cleaning purposes as long as all traces are brushed out before you enter the ring.

Check that your Whippet's teeth are clean. If your dog is properly fed and given something hard to chew, there should be no problem. If tartar starts to build up, you should get the teeth properly cleaned by a vet. In time, you may gain enough experience to do it yourself.

I believe that correct, regular exercise is very important to keep your Whippet in top condition for the show ring. Some coursing enthusiasts in Britain blame poor movement in the breed on breeders who show their dogs rather than work them. This is rubbish! I have never raced or coursed any of my dogs, and I always present them in fit show condition. They have two miles road walking every day, plus a twenty minutes free run in a safe field.

If you follow the above tips you should have a Whippet in pristine condition. You will be proud of your dog in the show ring, and more importantly, you will be the owner of a happy and healthy dog.

JUDGING THE WHIPPET

To the newer judges, I would emphasise that you have to walk before you can run. You have to have a great love for your breed, and you must be hungry to gain as much knowledge as you can. Be prepared to serve your apprenticeship. Study the Breed Standard very carefully. If there is any part that you do not understand, do not be afraid to ask the more experienced people to explain it to you.

My feelings are that very few of the newer breeders and judges know what a good shoulder and front should look like. There is much talk about bone and substance – but what is meant by it? Too many people interpret substance as fat, and there are far too many fat Whippets being shown. No one wants to see every bone in a dog's body: there should be just the right amount of covering for the Whippet to present a picture of elegance, which is typical of the breed. The bone should not be fine or too heavy, and it should not be bladed or round. Correct bone is so important in the quality of the Whippet.

I believe that type is the most important attribute to look for. Without it, you have not got a Whippet. After assessing type, I look for quality and soundness. Type has nothing to do with the size of the Whippet. I would like to give as examples Ch. Deepridge Mintmaster, considered quite a large dog in his time, but his type and quality were an example to all, and also the lovely Ch. Laguna Ravensdowne Astri, who had type, quality and soundness in

Two of the breed's most respected judges: Miss I.B. Clay (Tantivvey) is pictured left and Mrs Dorit McKay (Laguna) is on the right. I am handling Ch. Novacroft Madrigal.

The prospective judge must be prepared to serve their apprenticeship in the breed in order to give a knowledgeable and objective assessment of every dog in the class. On this occasion I had the honour of judging the two breed record holders: Ch. Nutshell of Nevedith (bitch) and Ch. Tilegreen Tornado.

abundance. If these two Whippets were to grace the rings of today it would be like comparing Dresden china to Staffordshire pottery.

I do not think that anyone should contemplate judging the breed at the lowest level without having had at least five years experience of showing and breeding top-class Whippets. If you have never had a good example of the breed yourself, how can you be expected to judge other people's dogs? Dog showing is a very expensive hobby, and exhibitors deserve to have their dogs judged by someone very conversant with the breed – not by someone who wants the Whippet to be another string to their bow.

It is preferable if your first judging appointment is outside your own area. It is far better to judge an entry that is fresh to you, rather than one where you know all the dogs – and all the

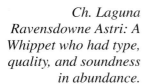
Ch. Laguna Ravensdowne Astri: A Whippet who had type, quality, and soundness in abundance.

Crufts 1994: Roma Wright–Smith's Ch. Silkstone Jewel in the Crown, Best of Breed and Reserve in the Hound Group.

exhibitors! The judge should always look clean and smart, and be conversant with ring procedure. Every dog in the class must be given the same time, and you must be tolerant of novice exhibitors and dogs attending their first show. You should be prepared to put both dogs and handlers at their ease, and never make anyone look foolish. You should always be looking to advance and promote the breed; you must never be side-tracked by personal ambitions.

If you make a good job of judging, you will be asked to officiate again. Do not be in too much of a rush to graduate to the big shows. Take your time to gain in confidence and experience. We are guardians of the breed for such a short time and we owe it to the breed to do our very best for future generations.

Chapter Six

THE PRINCIPLES OF BREEDING

THE PRINCIPLES OF INHERITANCE

The science of heredity, called genetics, is a new and rapidly growing branch of the biological sciences – those sciences which are concerned with living organisms. It is probably the most important of them all, for it deals with life itself. The name 'genetics' was coined because the unit of heredity was given the name of 'gene' (from the Greek 'genos' meaning a race). The gene is the hereditary factor which passes direct from parent to child and forms the sole connecting physical link between one generation and the next.

There are thousands of genes in every individual and they transmit the entire inheritance. They are carried on bodies called chromosomes, rather after the fashion of beads on a string. Both chromosomes and genes occur in pairs, one member of each pair being derived from the male parent, the other from the female. Theoretically, inheritance comes in equal amounts from both parents, but in effect, this is not the case.

When a dog and a bitch are mated the minute sperm of the dog unites with the egg of the bitch at fertilisation to produce the new individual. Theoretically, the union of two cells should give a double cell, twice the size of the two which formed it, with twice the amount of cell contents, including chromosomes and genes. However, the sperm and the egg are in effect only half cells: they are called gametes, and each possesses only half the normal number of chromosomes and genes. This process of cell division is a complicated process known as meiosis.

Before fertilisation takes place, the chromosomes – and the genes they carry – divide. One member of each pair goes to form an individual puppy, along with the corresponding half from the second parent. The contribution from each parent is a sample half of its own inheritance. Chance determines which particular gene will pass into which puppy, and which gene from the other partner will join it to become the second member of the gene pair.

MENDELIAN GENETICS

Genes combine in many ways. In some gene pairs, one member is able to suppress the effect of its partner. This was the first genetic discovery of Mendel, the father of Genetics, long before the name 'gene' was attached to what Mendel called a 'factor' of inheritance, which he postulated from the results of experiments on plants. His work was forgotten for over forty years, until it was discovered about the beginning of this century. In the meantime,

Hillsdown Fergal: A highly influential sire.

Ch. Barmoll Bejapers: A top brood bitch for the Barmoll kennel.

Mark Mason.

English scientists had come to the same conclusions, though, owing to a knowledge of the cell and its behaviour by this time available but unknown in Mendel's day, they were able to go a stage further.

Mendel called his pair of factors, the one suppressing the other, dominant and recessive. It follows that the recessive gene could give no signs of its presence when combined with a dominant partner. However, when this gene pair divides, the dominant member goes to one puppy and the recessive to another, and their effects will be different according to whether the new members are dominant or recessive.

The dominant-recessive relationship is the cause of many hereditary characters, notably faults, but it is far from being the only method by which genes work. Some can suppress the action of genes with which they are not paired, others can be suppressed. If suppressors, they are termed epistatic, if suppressed, hypostatic. Genes can modify the effect of other genes without having any other action, genes can dilute the effect of other genes; single pairs of genes can produce their effect, groups of genes may be needed to produce effects. In fact there are many ways in which genes can combine, and many stages between the gene and the character for which it is responsible. The dominant-recessive relationship, so often thought of as being the most usual and the most important, is only one of many others.

ENVIRONMENT
A second great force has its share in influencing the effect of heredity: it is that of the external circumstances we call environment, which includes everything which influences life and development, including events of the pre-natal period.We can take growth as an example of the action of environment on heredity. The hereditary pattern for this may be entirely favourable, but if the dog is starved of food of the right amount and quality, the hereditary pattern will be hampered and proper growth and development will not take place. On the other hand, the best environment will not correct a bad hereditary pattern of growth. We are now in a position to answer the questions put forward earlier.

RANDOM INHERITANCE
As we have seen, genes are distributed among the progeny at random and it would be possible for two litter-mates to differ very considerably in their inheritance. Related dogs are more alike on the whole: in spite of this random distribution of genes among progeny, they are more likely to possess genes in common because of the relationship. On the other hand, litter-mates may show dissimilar characters because the sample each received from both parents may be quite different on account of the separation of gene pairs at every mating and their recombination in the next generation.

MUTATIONS
Genes do not blend in the process of reproduction. Each maintains its own identity, and is passed on unchanged with every generation. The sole exception is that of a mutation. This is a sudden, usually permanent, change in a gene which alters its effect, so that the organism is different from the normal. Mutations are rare; they can be produced by radiation of various kinds. How the single gene behaves in the next generation may depend on the second gene of the pair, inherited from the second parent.

INHERITED CHARACTERISTICS

TEMPERAMENT
A fundamentally nervous temperament must be regarded as hereditary. It is true that nervousness in Whippets, as in other breeds, may be brought about by bad management and rough handling, but the hereditary nervous Whippet is frightened from the beginning, and remains so, however well-treated. Fortunately, these Whippets are rare, but they are a pitiful sight. Even small puppies will display fear for no apparent reason, and will refuse to respond to friendly advances.

In later life, this temperamentally unsound dog will be terrified of normal everyday experiences, which the typical, even-tempered Whippet takes in its stride. Such temperaments are as great a handicap to the pet dog as they are to those which are shown, and every attempt should be made to eradicate them from stock of every kind. Animals displaying these faults should not be used for breeding.

CRYPTORCHIDISM

This refers to the failure of testicles to descend into the scrotum. The word does not describe a dog in which one or both testicles are absent from the body. One or both testicles may be retained within the abdomen, in the kidney region (where they take origin in pre-natal life) lower down in the abdomen, or in the inguinal canal. If one testicle is present in the scrotum and the other retained, the dog is a one-sided or unilateral cryptorchid; if both are retained, the dog is a double or bilateral cryptorchid.

A bilateral cryptorchid dog is sterile, as the higher temperature within the abdomen reacts unfavourably on the sperm manufactured in the testicle. Moreover, there is a tendency for malignant changes to take place in an undescended testicle, in dogs as in humans. The normal disposition of the animal often changes, probably as a result of the changes in normal sex hormones made in the testicles. Unilateral cryptorchids (or monorchids) are able to sire normal litters, but they are not allowed to be shown.

It seems certain that bitches can carry the gene for the defect, though for obvious reasons they cannot display it. The exact method of its inheritance has not yet been firmly established, and views on the question differ. However, any factor which tends to diminish fertility, or could do so, is a potential danger to the breed in which it occurs. As far as Whippets are concerned, we have very few dogs which are not entire. Puppies normally show evidence of testicles soon after birth, by slight swellings on the scrotal sac on both sides, and these swiftly develop into normal testicles, located in the correct position.

INBREEDING

There are few subjects which breeders discuss more often or with greater fervour than the part breeding can play in the improvement of type in pedigree dogs. The opinions expressed as regards the value or danger of inbreeding, as compared with line breeding and outcrossing, show the widest divergences. Some breeders look upon inbreeding – the mating of very close relatives, mother to son, father to daughter, brother to sister, etc. – as an evil to be avoided at all costs, contending that it must bring disaster and ruin in its wake. Others claim that it is the only sure road to success for those whose aim it is to build up a strain which can be relied on to breed true for the breed points required.

In fact, it is equally illogical to suppose that, in itself, inbreeding is either a malignant force or a sovereign remedy for all the difficulties which lie in the breeder's path. Inbreeding is simply a means of sorting out the virtues and faults inherent in a strain or family. Whether its results are good or bad depends entirely on the type of the stock that is subjected to its influence, and the care with which it is applied.

The breeding together of more distantly related individuals such as cousins, uncle and niece, half-brother and half-sister and so on, is referred to as line breeding. Many people who are strongly opposed to inbreeding are great advocates of line breeding, yet there is no essential difference between the two. Line breeding is merely a mild, or less intense, form of inbreeding.

GENETIC PURITY

Genetically, most of the points we seek to obtain in show stock are represented by dominant genes, while the unwanted characteristics, which we call faults, are produced by recessive genes. In any breed of dog, two near relatives are likely to have more genes in common than are two unrelated individuals, and the closer their relationship, the more alike genetically they are likely to be. The most direct method of producing genetic purity in a strain is, therefore, by inbreeding.

However, it must be remembered that genetic purity applies to faults as well as to virtues. Inbreeding will fix both good and bad points, and it will bring to light any weakness or defect which may be dormant in the parents. The first visual results of inbreeding may, therefore, be disappointing. Litters born to an inbred mating may show some, possibly many, faults which were not apparent in either of the parents, but the genes for the development of those defects must have been carried by both sire and dam. Inbreeding cannot create either good or bad points. It can only make visible what is present, though hidden, in the animals that are mated.

It is a common fallacy to suppose that such failings as loss of vigour, weak pigmentation, impotence, sterility, susceptibility to infection, mental degeneration, loss of size, or bad temperament, can originate through inbreeding. If these or any other defects appear in inbred stock it is because the parents carry the hereditary factors responsible for these conditions. The emergence of faults through the coming together of recessive genes can, of course, occur in litters bred from unrelated parents, but inbreeding certainly increases the risk. Any characteristics, whether physical or mental, can be fixed in, or eliminated from, a strain by inbreeding. Physical or constitutional strength, fertility, fearlessness, size or high intelligence and trainability may be inbred into a strain as surely as may such points as length of head, ear shape, eye colour or coat texture. This fact is very apt to be ignored by those who seem to regard inbreeding as being inevitably associated with degeneration.

If the early results of inbreeding are disappointing the remedy is not to go over to outcrossing – the breeding of two completely unrelated animals – but to continue to inbreed, with drastic weeding out of all faulty progeny as it appears. The main reason why inbreeding is often condemned by breeders who have only slight experience of it, is that they have failed to persevere long enough for the benefits, which might have been derived, to become apparent, or they have not been ruthless enough in discarding all faulty or weakly puppies in the litters bred. If vigorous culling is practised in the early stages, inbred stock will become increasingly more uniform, both in appearance and genetically, in later generations, so that a true breeding line of high-quality, typical animals may be established.

It is useless to embark on a programme of inbreeding with chance-bred or mediocre stock. *At every mating the animals chosen must be of high quality and free from any serious hereditary defects.* Unless material of this calibre is available, efforts should be concentrated on building up a stock of sound, typical individuals by outcrossing, line-

Am. Ch. Starline's Claim To Fame: Winner of the 1994 AWC Specialty and seven All Breed Best in Shows. Number one Whippet bitch in the US for 1991, 1992 and 1993.

breeding and selection. The object of inbreeding is to produce a strain of animals all conforming closely to a desired pattern. The longer inbreeding is continued, the more alike its products will become. In time it will be effective in fixing all the qualities inherent in a strain, both good and bad. If selection is applied with care and within wide enough limits in each generation, only the good points will be stabilised. However, if faults are unknown, overlooked or ignored in the animals bred from, they, too, will be fixed in the strain and further inbreeding will cause deterioration.

LINE BREEDING

In line breeding the mated animals are less closely related, so that the resemblance of offspring to parents will probably be less strongly marked than in closely inbred stock. Genetic purity and physical uniformity will also take longer to achieve, but though it is slower in fixing desirable qualities than inbreeding, line-breeding is also less likely to expose faults. For that reason, where immediate results are of more importance than the ultimate establishing of a genuine true-breeding strain, it may be considered preferable and safer than inbreeding.

It should, however, be understood that anything which may be gained through line-breeding may be obtained more quickly and more directly by inbreeding. The point to bear in mind is that the higher the general quality of a strain, the closer it may be inbred without ill effects – always providing that precautions are taken to weed out every puppy which fails to come up to a required standard. To attempt to initiate a programme of inbreeding with inferior stock or to continue with it when a fault shows signs of becoming fixed in the strain is to court certain disaster.

OUTCROSSING

An outcross – the breeding together of two unrelated animals – should only be made for a special purpose. The belief that a change of blood must in all cases be salutary, after inbreeding has been practised for a few generations, is, in my opinion, mistaken. If, through lack of care in selection, or from other causes, a recessive fault becomes widespread in a strain, it may be necessary to resort to an outcross in order to bring in the dominant gene to correct it. The snag is that, however carefully an outcross is chosen, the animal is almost certain to bring in not only the genes desired, but other factors that are not wanted. An outcross dog or bitch will probably be genetically impure for several of the qualities for which a high degree of genetic purity has been established in the line. Therefore certain recessive genes will be passed on to any progeny. An outcross should be regarded as an experiment, and in a well-established strain should not be made without good reason.

There are times when outcrossing may be imperative, as when a fault or weakness occurs repeatedly in members of a certain family or strain; but every effort should be made to see that the animal used brings in as few alien traits, or genetic impurities, as possible. The best way to ensure this is to try to find an individual which, though not closely related, carries some of the same foundation bloodlines as the strain with which it is to be crossed. In a small or numerically weak breed that may not be feasible, but in the more popular varieties, like Whippets, a breeder resorting to indirect line-breeding, as opposed to inbreeding in the restricted sense, may be able to obtain the desired results with less risk than by a more dramatic outcross.

Having made an outcross, the next step is to breed back strongly to the original line. Except in very exceptional circumstances this is the only safe course to follow, once the purpose of outcrossing has been achieved. Only in this way can the genetic purity previously established in a valuable strain be maintained.

Chapter Seven

THE STUD DOG

MAINTAINING QUALITY

I have already dealt fully with the question of selecting breeding stock, and therefore I need only emphasise the importance of keeping stud dogs of the highest quality. In fact, a great many small breeders never keep a stud dog of their own – and this applies to all breeds, not only to Whippets. There are very few really influential stud dogs around at any one time – those prepotent males who are capable of passing on their virtues when mated to many different bitches. These dogs are the ones that shape the breed over many generations, and they are highly valued by all breed enthusiasts.

There is absolutely no point in keeping a stud dog that is second-rate, third-rate, or even worse. This type of dog is detrimental to the breed as a whole and spells doom for the future of his owner's kennel. Keeping an inferior dog is a waste of time and money. The breeder cannot rest content if a stud dog consistently sires pet puppies. This is simply not good enough. The market for pet Whippets is not of any commercial significance, and demand is never very strong. Therefore devotees of the Whippet never breed with the pet market in mind. Our aim is to breed for Championship show winners, and nothing less. However, this is easier said than done. There is no question that the top breeders have tremendous knowledge and experience, but even with all that know-how, a proportion of the puppies produced will not be good enough for showing. They make delightful pets and there are plenty of them about – there is certainly no need to set out to breed them.

STARTING A STUD DOG'S CAREER

Assuming you have either bought, or bred a dog who is destined to become a stud force in the kennel, you must now provide the environment and conditions which will help you to get the best from your dog. In most kennels, a stud dog is used on the home stock and offered at public stud in the expectation that it will earn some revenue in the form of stud fees. How early in life can such a dog be started on his career? Nature and Kennel Club rules take care of this question, as the dog will not be capable of serving a bitch until such time as it is right to let him do so. If the dog appears keen and able to mate, it will probably do him no harm to let him serve one bitch, even if he is still young. He should, however, be very carefully and patiently handled, and every precaution should be taken to make sure that he is not hurt or frightened. Ideally, the bitch should be an experienced brood, so that she

Ch. Play A While at Peperone: Top Whippet in Sweden in 1989, he became Top Stud Dog in 1993, and is the dominant stud force at the present time.

knows what is happening and does not try to snap at the dog, or make things more difficult for him. Dogs vary greatly in their approach to the reproductive act, and some mature much more rapidly than others. We get the cocky fellow who will ape his elders by lifting his leg when the other puppies are still babyish, and he takes an interest in females at four or five months old. However, the puppy should be at least eight or nine months, and preferably ten or eleven months, before his 'manhood' is utilised. Some youngsters are well over a year old before they take an interest in the opposite sex, and they require a lot of patient manipulation in order to mate a bitch for the first time.

HANDLING A STUD DOG

The most normal course of events is for the young, novice stud dog to mate the bitch, but to take his time about it. However, an early lesson in breeding is that there is no such thing as a 'normal' situation. All dogs are individuals, and therefore all dogs react differently to a given situation. A very keen young puppy may go about the task of mating with the skill and aplomb of an old hand, while another may refuse bitch after bitch, and then suddenly decide to mate one which, so far as can be seen, is no more receptive or attractive than those he has rejected. It is tiresome if a dog remains apathetic over his bitches when it is specially desired to mate him, but as long as he is entire, he is almost sure to oblige at some time.

The experienced brood bitch will certainly be more amenable and easier to mate than a maiden bitch. Furthermore, if there are no puppies as a result, you will know that, while it may be "just one of those things", the bitch is a proven breeder and so it might be the fault of the dog. If a maiden bitch and an untried dog are mated unfruitfully, it could be that either the bitch or the dog is barren, but as both have not previously produced young, there is no guidance as to where the blame may lie. The ideal bitch to try with an up-and-coming stud dog is one of his own kennel companions. He will not feel strange with her, and with both animals on the spot, you will be able to put them together when the bitch seems perfectly

Ch. Lowglen Newbold Cavalier: A highly infuential sire in Britain.

Diane Pearce.

ready. A youngster can mess about and waste much of his energies and enthusiasm trying to mate a bitch who is not quite ready. A visiting bitch is often nervous, uneasy and under a strain. She will snap at anybody or anything. There have been instances where promising youngsters have had a stud career cut short before it even began by unfortunate early experiences when bitches have frightened and upset them.

If the first bitch has to be one from outside the home establishment, an experienced owner will probably manage to bring her when she is standing to a dog and at just the right stage in her oestrum or heat. A beginner in the dog breeding game may make the mistake of coming too early or, worse still, too late, especially if there is no male dog available that can be used to test the bitch's reaction. It is not at all easy to know the perfect time to take a bitch to the sire, but it is better to err on the early side. You must choose a quiet spot for the service to take place, well away from the other dogs. If the same place can be used every time it is an advantage, as very small things, such as unaccustomed surroundings, can put a dog off. Do not embark on the task in the dining-room (although I know people who always arrange the stud work there) – the stud dog should be able to run about and lift his leg if he wants to. It is the natural thing for him to do when he is courting a bitch, and it would be very unkind to scold him for what is the normal behaviour.

Allow the dog and bitch to play together for a minute or two, but keep a sharp eye on the bitch in case she is going to growl and snap. When the pair seem to be getting on well together, put a collar on the bitch so that she can be held when the dog mounts her. If she is inclined to collapse under his weight, put the other hand gently under her tummy. If she keeps sitting down, the dog will wear himself out and get discouraged.

As you support the bitch, check to see if she is the right height for the dog. If she is not, just put a bit more pressure on her tummy and push her up. Should the bitch become very fidgety or inclined to snap, it is best to get a second person to help. In fact, it is just as well to have the help of a reliable assistant throughout the proceedings. One person can hold the bitch by the collar and soothe her, while the other can look after the rear end, holding her tail to one side, keeping her standing firmly on all four legs, and getting ready to hold the male in position once he gets going.

Once the dog has made contact, make sure you hold the bitch and the dog firmly. If either jumps away, they may spoil everything. When the dog has 'tied' inside the bitch, he can either remain where he is, on top of the bitch, or be allowed to slide gently down. Help him lift his leg over, so he can stand comfortably. The bitch may need a bit of support, and this should be given by placing your hand under her tummy. It is absolutely essential that you do not let her pull away from the male – she could quite easily rupture him.

The male's ejaculation occurs in three parts. The first fluid is a mixture of semen and any other residue that was in the penis, and this is passed within the first few seconds. The sperm is passed within one or two minutes of penetration when the male is still thrusting, and this is helped on its way by the seminal fluid which is passed during the tie. The tie is the result of the swollen bulb, located at the base of the penis, being held in place by the muscles of the bitch's vagina. The tie may last for just a minute or two, or it can go on for as long as an hour. An average tie lasts about fifteen to twenty minutes. The pair cannot part until the swollen bulb decreases in size.

SLIP MATINGS

A mating can be successful if the male and female fail to tie – known as a slip mating – contrary to popular belief. Even if the pair do not tie, the vital sperm has still been passed to the female in the first few minutes of the mating. All it means is that the male's swollen gland has not gone into the bitch with the rest of his penis. In this situation, the best course of action is to attempt to hold the two animals together. This should be done by pressing firmly at the dog's back-end with one hand, and placing your other hand under the bitch's back legs. Then, with two fingers, grasp the back of the dog's swollen bulb on each side,and repeatedly press it and let go, with a scissor-like action. This has the effect of replacing the muscle contractions of the bitch.

When the pair part, lift the dog down. If it has been a slip mating, lift the bitch up by the back-end, with her hindquarters higher than her head, keeping her in this position for a minute. If there has been a tie, you do not need to lift the bitch.

AFTER THE MATING

The bitch should then be returned to her kennel and kept quiet for about an hour before letting her out to relieve herself. Passing urine immediately after mating can prejudice the chance of puppies. However, the stud dog should have a good run and be allowed to make himself comfortable before he, too, returns to his kennel. It is better not to put him in a run or pen with other males, even if they are ordinarily good friends. The scent of a bitch in season will be very noticeable, and it may result in the stud dog being attacked by jealous competitors. A few hours later he can go out with the others as usual, and the scent will no longer be obvious to them.

I like my bitches to have two services, forty-eight hours apart. Others, including some veterinary surgeons, believe that one mating is sufficient. This is obviously a matter of opinion, and every breeder pursues the policy that has proved most successful for their kennel. There is much to be taken into consideration when mating valuable dogs and bitches, and tactful handling is essential. It is too often assumed that a successful mating can be achieved by putting a male and a female in a run and leaving them alone for the rest of the day. Apart from the uncertainty of not knowing if a mating has taken place, the dog can be seriously injured if he effects a tie with a restless bitch. It is not only unwise, but it is cruel to leave a dog and a bitch in season alone, without the help of a skilled attendant.

THE STUD DOG'S WORKLOAD

How often can a stud dog be used? This is a difficult question to answer, because some dogs are more robust and fertile than others. It is also a worth bearing in mind, that stud work is never regular. Even if the dog was patronised extensively, he could only cope if the matings were regularly spaced, two per week, with two or three days between each.

Nature being what it is, things never work out like this, and so it is impossible to plan a regular schedule of stud work. Although bitches come into season all the year round, there are periods when a lot of bitches come in season at about the same time. This is especially true of the weeks beginning in late December and extending into April. A popular stud dog can receive applications from the owners of four or five bitches, all of whom want to use him within the space of a few days. Then there may be a gap of three weeks or more when there are no further requests for his services.

It is therefore impossible to be dogmatic about a stud dog's capabilities. It is probably fair to say that a vigorous youngster, in fine condition, should be able to serve three or four bitches within a week – provided none of them is especially difficult to mate, and provided the dog can be rested the week before, and the week after this busy period. If the dog has had a struggle to serve one of the bitches, and it has been a long and wearing business, then it is questionable whether he should be allowed to try again until he has had some days of complete rest; this applies equally to a mature dog. A puppy embarking on his career at stud should not have more than one or two bitches per month until he is about fourteen months old. By the time a healthy dog is eighteen months of age, he should be perfectly capable of dealing with any normal number of applications for his services.

THE STUD FEE

Stud fees are charged for the use of a dog, and the fee covers the actual act of service, not the result, as many people suppose. However, there is a moral responsibility on the part of the sire's owner to do everything possible to ensure a fruitful union. The dog should be fit and well, and fed a top-quality diet. He should never be over-worked, and the mating should be attended by a competent handler. The bitch should also be given every care, both before and after the coupling. If there are no puppies as a result of the visit, the stud fee is not returnable, either in whole or in part. Most stud dog owners will agree to a free service at the next heat. This is regarded as customary rather than obligatory.

It is advisable to ask the stud dog owner to stipulate the conditions for bitches to be accepted for a booking. The dog's owner should provide these, either printed on the pedigree card or on a separate sheet. This means there can then be no arguments regarding payment of the fee. The amount charged for the fee should be based on the scale of stud fees common throughout the breed. The sire's show success can be taken into consideration, as well as the quality of his pedigree. If a dog has bloodlines that include very scarce and sought-after strains, he could command as high a fee as a reigning Champion, even if he has not done as much winning himself. Never make the mistake of charging too little There is hard work and responsibility involved in standing a dog at stud, and it can also be very stressful and time-consuming.

PUPPY DEALS

All owners of stud dogs are asked from time to time if they are willing to take a puppy from the prospective litter in lieu of cash payment at the time of mating. A few owners, particularly those who do not do much breeding and therefore have few, if any, bitches of their own, will welcome this type of arrangement. I have done this on occasion, and always been pleased with the deal. The advantages of such agreements can bebeneficial to both parties. The owner of the stud dog can pick up a very good puppy sired by his dog, and the breeder will have the satisfaction of seeing the bitch's offspring making a name in the ring, or as the new stud dog in a prestigious kennel.

THE UNDERSTUDY

If you are keeping a stud dog, it is advisable to have an understudy. Many dogs have strongly individual ideas and may refuse to mate a bitch who is apparently ready and willing. By this stage, it may be too late for the owners to rush the bitch to another dog, so it is useful to have another male available, preferably of equal merit. The understudy can be shown the rejected bitch, and if he, too, is disinterested, it is obvious she is either not ready or has gone past her prime time for mating. On the other hand, if the understudy is keen and anxious to mate, then you will still be able to achieve a successful mating. Dogs are all individuals, and sometimes a male will refuse to perform for no apparent reason. It is advisable to ask the owners of the bitch if, in the event of the chosen sire refusing to mate, they are agreeable to the bitch being tried with another dog in your kennel.

KEEPING RECORDS

Keep a record of all the bitches sent to your stud dog. Printed books of stud service receipts, with counterfoils, are satisfactory, and leave room for the most important details: registered name of bitch, dates of service(s), name and address of owner, etc. I also include the names of the bitch's sire and dam, and I make a note as to whether the service was straightforward, or if there were any complications. This information often comes in useful at a later date.

In conclusion, if you are lucky enough to get a good male puppy by your beautiful stud dog, do not be persuaded to part with him too easily. So many people live to regret the fact that they have dwelt too much in the present, without giving sufficient thought to the future. It is good to have another young stud dog growing up, regardless of how well his sire is doing. There is nothing sadder than to see a kennel fading out of the limelight because it has failed to produce a succession of good dogs to keep it to the fore.

Chapter Eight

THE BROOD BITCH

SELECTION

A good brood bitch is a pearl above price. She is to be the rock on which we build, and because of her importance, much thought must be given to her selection. It is always worth remembering that all the top kennels were built on good brood bitch lines.

Whatever size she is, the brood bitch should be typical, and she should excel in some of the more important breed characteristics. It is even better if she is from a free whelping line – not that Whippets are prone to whelping complications, but it is worth checking. The bitch should be maintained in good condition. She must be carefully fed and exercised. She must never be allowed to get lean or ribby. Equally, she must not be overfed so that she becomes fat.

Bitches can come into season at any time after they are six months old, although most Whippets have their season nearer twelve months of age. This being the case, the next

Ch. Oakbark Generation Girl: Top brood bitch 1992. A good brood bitch is a pearl above price.

season will be at eighteen to twenty months – and I believe that this is the best age to mate a Whippet for the first time. There is a theory that the muscles are pliable in a young female, and that this enhances the chances of easy whelping.

Many people believe that the bitch should not be bred from until her third heat, giving her the time to achieve mental and physical maturity. However, although there are differing views about the best time to mate a maiden bitch, everyone is unanimous in agreeing that it is a risk to wait until a bitch is three years or over before she is mated for the first time. It is a definite risk to wait until a Whippet bitch is four years old before she whelps her first litter.

THE IN-SEASON BITCH

Under normal circumstances, a Whippet bitch ovulates on approximately the thirteenth day of her season, but some bitches will be willing to stand from the tenth day, following the first signs of oestrum. The first day the bitch shows colour is counted as the first day of the season. You will get some warning that a bitch is coming into season, as she is likely to pay more attention to her hindquarters, and she will squat to urinate more frequently.

Even if you pin-point the first day of the season, it is far from easy to know which is the best day for mating your bitch, particularly if you have no male dogs on the premises to keep you informed. This also poses problems for the stud dog's owners, since they cannot be certain of the days when their dog's services will be required. Because of this uncertainty, owners should always make arrangements to take the bitch to the selected dog well in advance of the day when she is expected to be ready. It is best to write or telephone when the first signs of a red discharge are observed. If a likely day is fixed, perhaps the twelfth day, this can be put forward or postponed when the bitch's behaviour gives a clue as to the way things are working out.

Most bitches show a decided swelling of the vulva for one or two days, and then this is followed by a discharge which resembles blood. This can be observed for a few days or for over a week, and then it will change in colour: it will no longer be bright red, but a sort of watery pink. At this stage, or very soon after, it is most likely that the bitch will be ready and eager to mate, and she should be introduced to the dog without further delay.

Some bitches discharge less than others and many are fastidious in their habits, constantly licking and cleaning themselves, which makes it hard to check their progress. It helps if you provide a clean white towel or piece of old sheeting for a bed-cover. Then every spot of discharge will be noticeable, and if the cover is changed daily and a fresh piece of material supplied, the subtle deviations in the colour and consistency of the mucus can be carefully checked.

While a bitch is attractive to the other sex from the first day to the last, she is unlikely to accept the dog for the first few days, nor is the dog very determined about serving her until she is nearly or completely ready. But there are exceptions to every rule, and it is best to be safe rather than sorry, so keep the bitch under careful supervision right from the start. She should not be allowed to roam in the garden unattended, even if it is fenced. Males are remarkably determined when they are aware of a bitch in season, and a dog is quite capable of jumping over a wall or digging underneath.

The risks of accidental matings are very real. Misalliances have been known and there have been cases when bitches have mated with dogs considerably larger than themselves, so it is best to be cautious. Keep the bitch shut up in her pen and behind doors; exercise her regularly but only on a lead. If several bitches live together they will play about, and when the bitch on heat shows signs of flirtatiousness with them, she is probably getting ready to visit the dog.

VISITING THE STUD DOG

It is customary for the bitch to visit the stud dog on his premises, and the most satisfactory arrangement is for the breeder to travel with the bitch. The mating can be supervised, the breeder is on hand to help, and, in most cases, the whole thing will be over within an hour and the bitch can be taken home. A mating that is conducted with the minimum of fuss is advantageous to both the dog and the bitch. It is less tiring, and less stressful, and therefore the chances of success are greater.

THE IN-WHELP BITCH

When she is home again, the bitch must be very carefully guarded for the remainder of her season, which may last another week or ten days. There is no need to alter the routine for the first month after mating, particularly as you do not know at this stage whether the bitch is in whelp. It is a mistake to begin stuffing a bitch with extra nourishing foods too early, for she will only get fat, which is something to be avoided at all costs.

After four or five weeks, there should be signs of pregnancy. There may be an obvious swelling of the abdomen or a slightly rounder appearance, which an observant owner will detect immediately after the animal has had a meal. At this stage the swelling becomes rapidly more obvious, and the protein in the diet can be increased. If the bitch enjoys raw meat, there is nothing better for her at this time.

Some bitches become very hungry when they are in whelp; others, who previously had good appetites, become rather indifferent feeders. The latter must be pampered and tempted with delicacies, because the bitch needs plenty of nourishment to enable her puppies to develop inside her without exercising a drain on her bodily resources. She also needs to build herself up so that she will have plenty of milk for her babies.

The average pregnancy lasts for sixty-three days. At the beginning of the last week of her pregnancy, the bitch should be offered a light milky breakfast in addition to her solid food. She may like to have meat divided into two small meals rather than one large meal. It may be advisable to give her a small dessert-spoonful of liquid paraffin daily for the last week only. Extras, such as calcium and bone meal, are not necessary for a normal Whippet bitch. These supplements can be given – in fact I know quite a few breeders who give them all the time – but I firmly believe that you have to breed for bone and substance; you cannot hope to provide it by means of supplements.

The exception is the bitch that is likely to suffer from eclampsia, a calcium deficiency condition which causes alarming convulsions that have been known to prove fatal. This may occur at any stage after whelping when the bitch is nursing her puppies. The signs are heavy panting, the bitch will be restless, constantly lifting her puppies, and her eyes will be glazed.

She will eventually go into a convulsion and probably die if she does not get veterinary attention immediately. It is essential that she receives an injection of calcium – she will usually make a swift recovery. The vet will also prescribe the best methods to try to avoid a recurrence of the trouble.

You must be prepared in case your bitch whelps early. Puppies can arrive alive and well any time from the fifty-seventh day. Puppies up to six days early usually do well, but any born eight days early have a poor chance of survival. The whelping box should be prepared well ahead of time, and the bitch should be encouraged to sleep in it for a week or two before her due date, then she will not feel strange when the times comes for her to settle down and have her puppies. It is essential to choose a quiet spot for the whelping. Many litters have been lost, especially when the bitch concerned is young and inexperienced, because other dogs have been allowed to interfere or well-meaning people have been too persistent in their attentions.

The whelping box does not need to be elaborate. A small wooden kennel or box, which allows plenty of room for ventilation, with a hinged side and lid is satisfactory. I like my bitches to whelp in the bedroom, where it is peaceful and quiet. Then, after two weeks, I move her to another room where there is more space for the puppies to move about when they get up on their feet.

WHELPING

The first signs that indicate whelping is imminent may vary, but probably the bitch will become fidgety, wander about, sit down and lick herself, and whine. She may ask to be let out, and will then want to come back in again almost immediately. She will try to pass urine frequently and look rather uncomfortable and worried. In between times she will tear at her bed, scratching it into heaps. It is therefore advisable to take away cushions, rugs or blanket, and to line the bed with a piece of clean bath towel on top of some thick newspapers. The bitch's temperature will also drop prior to whelping. The normal temperature is 101.5 degrees Fahrenheit, and this will drop to about 100 degrees in the last week of pregnancy. The final drop to 99 or 98 degrees usually occurs twenty-four hours before whelping.

The uneasiness and bedmaking can go on for an hour or two, or for most of the day or night. They are sure signs that labour is about to begin, and eventually the bitch will start to strain. She will become less excited, and may curl up in her bed. Straining will become more definite, and you may see the water bag – balloon-like in appearance – at the vulva. This will be swiftly followed by the arrival of the first puppy. If all is going well, the slimy, bluish tip of a puppy's nose will appear. Another heave and a grunt from the mother, with perhaps a quick cry of pain, and a puppy emerges.

A sensible bitch will seize it and in a most expert way chew, suck, and lick at the unattractive membrane which envelopes the puppy, pulling it away, and finally biting off the cord. The puppy, bounced about and pushed around, fills its tiny lungs with air and utters its first cry. If the bitch is at all slow about this then she must have help, otherwise the puppy will die. With the corner of a towel wipe the mucus away from the puppy's mouth and nose. Then dip your fingers in an antiseptic solution, and, using your thumbnail, rub the umbilical cord in a sawing motion. This should sever the cord, just as the bitch would do with her teeth. This should be done about one inch from the puppy's tummy. You should now rub the puppy dry and return it to the mother, or put it in a blanket inside a cardboard box and keep it warm.

If the jelly-like afterbirth or sac does not come away with the puppy, try not to break the cord until it is all pulled gently away. Some breeders like to remove afterbirths, but I allow my bitches to eat them. However, it is essential to watch the bitch to see if she has expelled the afterbirth. Retained afterbirths can be very dangerous, causing septicaemia in the uterus, and many bitches have been lost for want of a little extra care. If you suspect your bitch has retained an afterbirth, ask the vet to give her an injection, which will help her to contract the uterus and expel the afterbirth.

A bitch, particularly a maiden bitch, may have difficulty in expelling a puppy. If straining persists for over ninety minutes and there is no sign of a puppy, telephone the vet and seek advice. If the head of a puppy appears, it should be possible to take hold of it, masking the hand and fingers in a piece of clean towel so that a firm grip is ensured, and then to pull firmly downwards and under the bitch until the puppy emerges. Do not hurry this. Pull slowly and, if possible, time it from the moment when the bitch is straining.

Sometimes puppies come tail and back legs first, which is known as a breech presentation. It is often more difficult for a bitch to expel a puppy in this position, and it is also harder to help her as there is not much to grip on to. If a puppy is protruding, or if it can be felt with the tip of a very well-scrubbed and greased finger, it needs to be born quite quickly or it will die. If the bitch does not progress and if it does not seem possible to assist, a vet should be called. Delay at this stage is dangerous, as the other whelps waiting to be born may become distressed.

CAESARIAN BIRTH

When the puppies are all born, the bitch will usually settle down and lick and feed her family. She will welcome a long drink of warm milk and glucose. If it has been a tiring whelping, she will probably curl round and go to sleep. This relaxed attitude is generally a sign that there are no more puppies to come. The size of the bitch herself is no real indication, as she may look quite distended for some hours, and it takes a little time for the swollen uterus to contract and for her figure to return to something like normal. However, an experienced breeder can feel if there are any puppies still to come, so if there is any doubt at all, it is wise to ask the vet to call. If there is a chance of a puppy having remained behind, or if it is uncertain whether all the afterbirths were expelled with the puppies that have been born, the vet will give an injection which should help the bitch to expel any matter remaining in the uterus.

If the vet is not successful in delivering retained puppies with the aid of manual manipulation or an injection, it will be necessary to resort to either forceps or a caesarian operation. Most vets are reluctant to use forceps, as it is a difficult and dangerous business groping round in an effort to grasp the slippery pup, and yet not pinching the delicate organs inside the bitch herself. When forceps are used, it generally means a tight grip on the puppy while it is extracted, and more often than not it is badly injured. A caesarian operation is a better proposition, and modern anaesthetics and antibiotics have greatly minimised the dangers. At one time the chances of a bitch surviving the operation were not high, but now the whole thing is over in a couple of hours and the bitch should progress well and take good care of her puppies. She will probably be given one or two daily injections of penicillin, and her stitches will have to be taken out in a fortnight (fourteen days).

If a maiden bitch has ·to have a caesarian operation, she may come out of her deep sleep and be totally bewildered and confused by the litter of puppies which are squeaking all around her. She will shrink into a corner of her box, and the expression on her face will be one of utter revulsion. She may growl at the puppies. Not having had them naturally, she has no idea that they are hers. If this happens, the bitch will need a lot of reassurance and encouragement from someone she loves and trusts. The puppies must be helped to suckle from the bitch, and this will involve holding them, one by one, to a teat, pressing the little mouths open and encouraging them to hang on by themselves. It may be necessary to keep on doing this at regular intervals until the bitch accepts her litter. If she can be persuaded to lick them, the battle is won. You can encourage her to do this by squeezing out some milk from her teats on to a puppy, or smearing it with a little butter.

Once a Whippet takes charge of the puppies, she will be a model mother, but even so, it may be a matter of hours or even a couple of days before her milk flows freely. It often comes down slowly after an operation, or even when the birth has been normal, especially if the puppies are premature. Even if the teats seem dry, it is still important to keep on trying to get the litter sucking, because this stimulates the milk flow.

CARING FOR THE LITTER
Both mother and puppies should be kept warm; the room temperature should be maintained at 70-75 degrees Fahrenheit. Remember, the puppies have just come from a snug, dark, cosy place, and if a newborn whelp is allowed to get cold, it is extremely difficult to restore heat into its tiny body. Because of this, many breeders take each puppy as it is born and place it in a flannel-lined box by the stove, preferably with a well-covered hot-water bottle or heating pads under the blanket for the puppies to crawl and lie on. When the bitch has finished whelping and has been given a clean dry bed, she can have all the babies back again. However, a few bitches become agitated and upset if the puppies are removed. If this happens, leave one puppy with the bitch in the whelping box, and the others can be removed to the warmth and safety of your puppy box. Be sure to let the bitch out to make herself comfortable. She will want to do this every few hours, for she will be most anxious to avoid soiling her bed and her precious babies. Do not let her stay out more than a minute or two – you do not want her or the new family to catch cold. The mother will not require her normal exercise until the puppies are beginning to grow up, but as soon as they leave the nest and start to toddle around, she will tend to be less solicitous, more prepared to leave them for short intervals, and will probably enjoy a daily walk. It will not hurt the pups if she is away from them for twenty minutes or so, and it makes a change for the dam.

As the puppies are weaned, the bitch will spend longer and longer periods away from them but, unlike bitches of many other breeds which become bored with their offspring at a very early stage, the Whippet mother will usually remain devoted to them for weeks or months, often for ever. She remains interested in her puppies, appears to know them and to

Hillsdown Mollie with her litter of puppies. Generally, Whippets have few problems when it comes to whelping or nursing a litter.

single them out for attention, even when she has been away from them for a considerable time. She will run to them, push them with her nose, lick them, and show every sign of delight at being reunited with her treasures.

POST-NATAL CARE

Many bitches, especially those which have been properly and generously fed, will leave a litter looking in perfect show condition. Others, and this is not necessarily any reflection on the care they have received, come away from their puppies looking very thin and poor. This type seem to pass on all the nourishment to their puppies without retaining enough for themselves, but they soon regain condition when lavishly fed and provided with a tonic. In all cases, it takes a few weeks for the milk glands to dry up and the pendant breasts to tighten, so very few show bitches are ready for the ring until some time after they have left a litter.

The condition of a dam when she has finished with her puppies must determine the question of when she should be mated again. If she has had a big litter, I would leave a gap of eighteen months, which gives the bitch ample time to recover, and it also gives you the opportunity to see how the puppies grow on and develop.

Chapter Nine

REARING A LITTER

STARTING WEANING

The stage at which weaning should begin is dictated by the amount of milk the dam is giving to her babies and this, in turn, is governed by her own state of health and by the number of whelps she is rearing. A bitch with a single puppy, irrespective of her condition, will probably continue to provide milk until the pup is at least six to eight weeks old. A bitch with several puppies may have a rapidly diminishing milk supply at any time from about three and a half to four and a half weeks following the birth of the litter, and this is very likely if she herself is debilitated. As soon as the bitch is conscious that she has insufficient nourishment for her babies, she may growl or snap at them when they try to suckle. This is a sign that the puppies must learn to lap, or they will have their growth impeded. Some bitches start the weaning process themselves by eating their own food and almost immediately vomiting it among the puppies so that they may eat it. Unfortunately, if the bitch has been fed meat in fairly large pieces, the puppies will choke or make themselves sick when they try to swallow it, so the habit is not one to be encouraged. If the bitch vomits her food for her litter, she should be kept away from them for a couple of hours after feeding time. Obviously, the perfect time to start weaning a litter is well before they begin to be a drain on their mother; so as soon as they can be persuaded to take an interest in milk and meat, these should be offered to them.

GIVING SOLIDS

The best-quality raw beef is the safest food to offer in the early days of weaning, and this will need to be scraped. To do this, take a chunk of meat weighing half a pound or more, and with a large sharp knife, scrape the meat, pressing the edge of the knife down firmly and drawing it towards you. As the fine pulp collects along the blade, put it aside in a saucer. When there is about two tablespoonfuls ready for each puppy, take the babies on your knee, one by one, and gently push the meat into the little mouths.

If the mother is still feeding them generously, the puppies will not be hungry and they may spit out the meat. If the puppies are still reluctant, keep the dam away for a couple of hours or so, and then try again. Continue to offer the puppies scraped meat in this manner twice daily until they fall on it greedily. The amounts can then be gradually increased until they are taking up to three good tablespoonfuls at a meal, according to size and appetite.

LEARNING TO LAP

While you are teaching the puppies to eat solid food, the bitch will still be having a good milky breakfast, and it is a good idea to try to interest the puppies in her dish each morning. They may not need much invitation, but will stumble into it to see what Mum is finding so attractive. Take each puppy gently, and press the mouth downwards until it touches the milk. Do not press too firmly, as this could result in the puppy getting liquid up its nose. The puppies will very soon learn to drink, and once they get going it is advisable to provide a separate saucer of milk for the litter, both morning and evening – and watch the mother to see that she does not drink her own and take theirs as well.

A BALANCED DIET

Offer the puppies scraped meat at midday and late afternoon, and provide milk for breakfast and supper, so that the puppies will be on four meals a day. If the puppies are thriving, you can replace the second meat meal with eggs, fish, or a manufactured puppy food. From this stage onwards, the diet can proceed on the lines suggested in Chapter Two: 'The Whippet Puppy'.

Always keep a careful watch on the litter for signs of tummy upsets, sickness or loose motions, and adjust the ration accordingly. Indigestion can generally be cured by withholding one of the solid meals, or by keeping the puppy on milk for a day and giving a little milk of magnesia.

There is nothing especially complicated or hazardous about feeding puppies. The main thing to remember is that the tiny stomachs should never be overloaded. The puppy requires ample, top-quality nutrients to achieve the correct grow and development, but this must never be offered in excessive quantities.When I start to rear my puppies, I divide the foods (eggs, fish, meat, etc.) into several meals a day. In this way, the digestive system is not overworked: it deals with one portion at a time and then prepares to receive another.

By the time the puppies are five weeks old, they will be getting very little of substance from their mother. However, there is no way of telling if the puppy is receiving sufficient nourishment, unless you detect loss of condition and unmistakable signs of hunger. By this time the puppy will have received a severe check in the growth process, which could have serious consequences. Therefore, I do not leave things to chance. I begin to supplement the puppy's feeds at an early date and gradually increase the quantities until the pup is independent of the dam.

Remember that a puppy is undergoing a transition from a milk diet to a solid diet – and the milk was served at exactly the right temperature, completely sterile, and at the perfect strength. The puppy must now learn to digest milk, which will probably be made up of different constituents, and get used to a variety of warm or cold solid foods of varying consistencies and textures – and all too often, of variable quality. The puppy's digestion faces quite a task, and this applies to a puppy of any breed. Whippets are no harder to wean or more difficult to feed than dogs of any other varietiy.

It is important to stress that only the best foods are suitable for puppies. Milk should be absolutely fresh, and meat must never be tainted, even though the adult dogs will eat it when it is a little high and be none the worse. Biscuit meals should be dry and crisp before soaking, and they should have a pleasant smell, without a hint of mouldiness. Musky dog biscuits should be thrown away – they are unsuitable for feeding to dogs of any age.

The preparation of the food is also important. Puppies are often greedy little creatures, especially when more than one is gathered round the dish. The competitive spirit prevails, and all concerned will grab, gulp, and push, trying to get as much as possible before the others eat the lot. In consequence, the puppies will bolt their food, and if it is fed to them in lumps, they will either choke, or if they swallow it, they will vomit it back again. Always keep an eye on puppies when they are eating. There may be a bully, or a puppy could start to choke. In this case, you must quickly intervene and use a finger to push the food down the puppy's throat, or to locate the obstruction and hook it out.

Very often a litter contains one puppy that is smaller and less robust than the others. While this can be due to a variety of causes, it may simply be that the puppy is being pushed out by the others and not receiving a fair share of food. In this instance, it is advisable to feed the pup separately, giving it a chance to catch up with the rest of the litter. Alternatively, if there is one pup which is getting the lion's share, feed this puppy alone, to give the others a better chance to thrive.

WORMING

Check the puppy for roundworms. These parasites are usually present to a greater or lesser degree in all puppies, whatever the breed. If left untreated a worm infestation can have a bad effect on the health of the dog, and may have a severe effect on the puppy's growth as well. A wormy puppy can be consuming plenty of nourishing food, but the worms will absorb much of the goodness and the dog will in fact virtually be starved. It is foolish to feed worms – the solution is to get rid of them. I worm my puppies at five weeks of age and then again at eight weeks. A worm-infested puppy is easily identified. The signs are leanness, a lack-lustre, rough-textured coat, a noticeable tendency to blow up after even a small meal, loose motions and motions composed of slimy mucus. In bad cases the puppy may suffer from convulsions. Sometimes worms are vomited one or more at a time.

The types of worming tablets available to dogs are many, and they have greatly improved over the years. Even a few years ago an effective worm dose involved hours of preparatory fasting, followed by a violent purge, which sometimes proved too much for a puppy already debilitated by the effects of the parasites. Nowadays there are a number of safe and effective preparations that can be given to very young dogs. Fasting is not necessary and the dog suffers no discomfort. It is best to consult your veterinary surgeon about worming your puppy, in order to get advice on the correct dosage according to the animal's age and weight.

When a puppy has been wormed, keep a careful watch, and if worms are passed, remove them and burn them. Worming is usually repeated after a week or two, in case any worm eggs have been left behind and developed since the others were expelled. After this, a dog kept under hygienic conditions should remain clear for a considerable time.

THE DEVELOPING PUPPIES

Whippet puppies are usually extremely tough, hardy and lively little creatures. Like most young animals, they require warmth and care in the nest as weaning progresses, and, hopefully, they will grow up to be strong, healthy dogs. Whippets are no more trouble to rear than any other breed of dog, and they are less prone to illness than a great many larger breeds in the canine race.

Puppies need opportunities for exercise, and they should be kept in a roomy pen where they can play and gambol. Freedom from draughts is a prime essential, and the puppies should have a warm kennel, containing some sort of bedding, so they can snuggle up and sleep when their games have tired them out. On warm summer days, the pen can be placed on the lawn, but if the sun goes down or a chill wind gets up, it is time to take the puppies indoors.

By the time they are four or five months old, the puppies will enjoy spells of freedom in the garden. Naturally, no puppy should be taken into streets or public parks until fully inoculated against the most prevalent canine diseases.

HAND-REARING

We have been happily assuming that the rearing of the puppies has followed the normal course, with the dam providing for her offspring in the early stages. Unfortunately, there are times when things go wrong, and supplementary feeding or total hand-feeding becomes necessary if the puppies are to survive. If a bitch whelps prematurely or if she had to have a Caesarian operation, it may be two or three days before her milk supply comes down. Very occasionally, a bitch may be lost through complications at whelping time, and in these tragic circumstances the puppies must be kept alive by artificial means.

For the first few hours after the puppies are born, the best substitute to offer is tepid boiled water containing a little glucose. The puppy will take only a few drops every two hours, administered to the tongue. A baby's feeder is ideal when the puppy is strong enough to suck. If the dam is not ill, the puppies should be put to her at frequent intervals. Each puppy in turn, must be held on to a teat and encouraged to suck. This stimulates the milk glands and helps to promote the flow, and perseverance usually produces the required result. If the bitch will lick and clean the babies, she must be allowed to do so, and if she appears to be accepting them and taking care of them, it is preferable to leave the puppies in her bed.

If the bitch is not responding to her puppies, or if you are caring for an orphaned litter, a cardboard box must be prepared. Wrap up a hot-water bottle in a couple of thicknesses of soft, clean towelling and put it in the box. Cover this with a clean piece of blanket and place the puppies on top. Cover the box with another piece of blanket, leaving a little space for air, and place the box in a warm spot, well away from draughts and out of the reach of other animals.

Fortunately, there are now many milk substitutes which can be used for hand-rearing puppies. These are specially formulated to be as similar to a bitch's milk as possible. It is important to make up the powder according to the manufacturer's instructions. This formula should be fed every two hours, night and day, increasing the quantity as the puppies demand. By the time the pups are a week old, they should be taking twice as much as they did at the start. However, a word of warning to the inexperienced: make haste slowly. Feed very very carefully, and let the puppy take plenty of time, thus avoiding indigestion and wind. The puppies must, of course, be kept very warm all the time.

Ch. Nutshell of Nevedith with a beautiful litter of puppies, sired by Ch. Pencloe Dutch Gold,
Crufts Best in Show winner.   *John Hartley.*

It cannot be too strongly emphasised that the milk mixture fed to puppies must be absolutely fresh. It can be mixed and kept in a refrigerator for short periods, but it is better to prepare it fresh each time a feed is due. The milk should be fed at a warm temperature, and you can test this by sprinkling a little on your hand. All utensils or feeders used should be boiled between meals, and they should be stored under a plastic basin or protected in some other manner from germs and dust. For the two-hourly interruptions through the night it is better to have a thermos flask, or a baby's bottle warmer, so that sufficient mixtures can be prepared to last until morning.

The mother normally cleans the puppies up as they feed, and if you are hand-rearing a litter, you have to take on the task of topping and tailing. You will need a supply of cotton-wool, a bowl of warm water, and a jar of Vaseline. Firstly, with a piece of damp cotton-wool, clean round the puppy's mouth, removing any food which may have spilled. Then gently smooth the puppy from the tail towards the tummy to encourage and assist the puppy to pass water and excreta. Then clean and dry, finishing off with a smear of Vaseline to prevent chafing.

The two-hourly schedule of feeding and cleaning must be continued for about ten days. By this stage the puppies will be taking more food, and the time between feeds can be extended to three hours, until they start to lap. As soon as this happens, night feeds can be suspended.

Nevedith Justa Jesta and Nevedith Justa Jenie: A son and daughter of Ch. Nutshell of Nevedith, sired by Ch. Pencloe Dutch Gold.

Day feeds should be continued as necessary, until the orphans are feeding well and are able to consume scraped raw beef. Food must be available for them to seek out during the night once they can lap and hand-feeding has been discontinued. At this stage, cereals can be added to the milk, and I give hard-boiled eggs (never uncooked eggs) to the puppies when they are about four to six weeks old.

It can be seen that hand-rearing puppies is time-absorbing, tiring and exacting, although it is also very rewarding. Even the weeks of sleepless nights seem worthwhile when you see a litter of healthy puppies playing happily together, which would have died had it not been for your efforts. Hand-reared puppies are always full of character, and never fail to have outstanding personalities. They have received so much love and attention, and they have had such gentle handling bestowed upon them from the start that they grow up with an engaging trust and dependence on human beings. Somehow this early and prolonged contact with human hands seems to stimulate their intelligence. This fact, in itself, is a further reward for the good-hearted individual who goes to the trouble of rearing them artificially.

It is not always necessary to take the puppies from the mother for good. Sometimes the inability to feed her puppies and her indisposition, whatever it may be, clears up after a few days and she is able and willing to accept the babies and to rear them herself. Provided the puppies have been kept warm and have been carefully fed until they go back to her, there should be no further problems. After all, the bitch is better equipped to look after the litter than the best-intentioned and most able foster-mother.

Chapter Ten

THE WHIPPET IN BRITAIN

From its humble beginnings, the Whippet is now one of the most elegant and popular breeds in the Hound Group, and frequently takes top honours at Championship Shows. During the last five years, we have seen Whippets break many records. The outstanding record of Ch. Selinko Another Lady who won twenty-five Challenge Certificates has been nearly doubled by the outstanding Ch. Nutshell of Nevedith with forty-four CCs – a record that is unlikely to be beaten. This Whippet has won more Groups and Best in Show awards than any other dog in the history of the breed, plus becoming the Dog of the Year All Breeds and Reserve Best in Show at Crufts 1990. The dog record of seventeen CCs held by Ch. Robmaywin Stargazer of Allways and the great Ch. Samarkands Greenbrae Tarragon for over twenty years, has now been taken by Ch. Tilegreen Tarnado's outstanding record of twenty-five CCs.

Ch. Martinsell Wild and Lonely has become the first blue Champion in the history of the breed, and his son, Ch. Ringmore Thief of Time, became the first blue and white male Champion. The Whippet Coursing Club's Moonlake Cup was won by Shirley Rawling's Ch. Chyton Copy Press – the second show Champion to win this honour, the first being Susan Baird's Ch. Sound Barrier. The outstanding Ch. Pencloe Dutch Gold had a spectacular year of show success in 1991, culminating in the breed's first-ever Best in Show at Crufts 1992. Both Nutshell and Dutch Gold won at Crufts under breed specialists – Nutshell won the Hound Group under Barbara Wilton-Clark, and Dutch Gold won the Group under Junes Minns and Best in Show under Ann Argyle. These famous judges of the Whippet must have thought these animals were truly outstanding to send them forward for top honours.

LEADING KENNELS
Over the last thirty-four years there have only been eight kennels that have owned or bred more than ten English Champions. They are:
Shalfleet (Barbara Wilton-Clark): 19
Oakbark (Mr and Mrs D. Meakin and Julie Greenwood Meakin): 18
Glenbervie (Mr A.B. Nicholson): 16
Dondelayo (Anne Knight): 13,
Nevedith (Editha Newton): 11
Harque (Ann Argyle): 11

Nimrodel (Mrs M. Lowe): 10
Lowglen (F. Nicholas): 10 – although three were owned in partnership, but campaigned as Lowglen.

Out of these, only the Nevedith, Oakbark and Nimrodel kennels are still actively breeding, although there are still Shalfleets with Cathy Thomas (Faracre), and I am now registered under the Dumbriton affix. I have gone into the top kennels in some depth to try to give newcomers to the breed an insight into how they developed their lines, with selective line breeding from the very best stock, and years of devotion to the breed.

HARQUE

Ann Argyle's latest Champion is Harque to Milo. He will be the last Champion from this famous kennel, as Ann is retiring from breeding due to ill health. Ann founded her kennel on Wingedfoot and Allways lines. During the sixties, there were five Champions bred from close line-breeding to these lines. The most famous was Ch. Harque the Lark. This bitch won nineteen CCs – a record at the time – two Supreme Best in Shows at General Championship Shows, two Reserve Best in Shows, and also Best in Show at the Hound Association.

In the seventies Ann used new blood and produced Ch. Harque to Pegasus (by Ch. Deepridge Mintemaster), and the Lark was mated to Ch. Dondelayo Buckaroo to produce the brindle bitch, Ch. Harque Yonder. By mating Yonder to Ch. Akeferry Jimmy, another close line was building up, and this mating produced the striking fawn and white parti-colour, Ch. Harque to Equerry, owned by Betty Beaumont. Equerry, mated to a Jimmy daughter, produced the lovely, quality fawn and white, Ch. Bonlouie Abalon Star, again owned by the Beaumonts.

In 1974 the Buckaroo son, Harque to Yeoman (litter brother to Ch. H. Yonder) was mated to H. to Wistful (also by Buckaroo) and produced Ch. H. to Coppelia. In 1980 Coppelia was mated to Equerry's brother, Harque to Eclipse of Aekla. This mating was to produce Ch. Harque to Huntsmen, the sire of the Newton's Ch. Huntress of Nevedith. Owing to Ann Argyle's great demand as an international all-round judge, over the last ten years her Whippets were not exhibited at many Championship Shows and not many litters were bred.

OAKBARK

The Meakins made up their first Champion in 1968 with the pale fawn dog, Ch. Oakbark Dondelayo Storming, bred by Bill Knight. Storming was by Dondelayo Desperado. a son of Ch. Courtney Fleetfoot of Pennyworth out of Nagrom Feola, a daughter of Ch. Playmate of Allways. Their foundation bitches were Laguna Lynda (by Ch. Laguna Ligonier) and Samarkands Sun Carona (by Ch. Samarkands Greenbrae Tarragon). Sun Carona was litter sister to Ch. Sun Courtier. There could not have been better lines to found a kennel, and the Meakins bred very wisely and were soon to produce Champions.

Laguna Lynda was mated to Ch. Sun Courtier to produce the very good stud dog, Oakbark Pyramid. Sun Carona was mated to Storming to produce Oakbark Michelle. Both Pyramid and Michelle, although never to gain their titles, were to produce Champions that were so important in the breed – not only for the Oakbark kennel, but for other Whippet kennels as

Ch. Oakbark Movie Queen (Ch. Towercrest Flarepath Taurus – Flarepath Aquaria): A fine representative of Oakbark breeding.

well. Two dogs were bought in that were to prove very influential. The first, Ch. Flarepath Tambillo Tarquin, came from the Flarepath kennel of Irene Wood, and he soon gained his title.

Tarquin did not cover many bitches before he was exported to the United States, but his breeding was superb – he was by Ch. Ravensdowne Bright Star out of a Ligonier daughter. Mated to Michelle, he produced Ch. Oakbark Micheala, owned by Marjorie and Des Howarth (Newbold). Micheala, when mated to Oakbark Pyramid, was to produce the two Newbold Champions – Kerry Gold and Muffin Man. With this breeding, it was not surprising that Muffin Man went on to sire Champions. Tarquin, when mated to Pyramid's litter sister, produced the two CC winning brothers, Lowglen Oakbark Masterminde and Oakbark Moonduster, both of whom went on to sire Champions out of Ch. Ravensdowne Bright Star daughters.

Masterminde was mated to the lovely Ch. Laguna Ravensdowne Astri, who produced a very good litter. One of the dogs went to Lowglen to become Ch. Flarepath Astrinought of Lowglen, and a bitch, Flarepath Aquaria, went to Oakbark. Like his sire, Tambillo Tarquin, Masterminde was exported. He went to the Martinique kennel, owned by Terry Crawley and Ian Doherty in Australia, where he proved such a great stud force. Moonduster was mated to Newbold Madalina, and out of this litter came the famous Ch. Beseeka Knight Errant of Silkstone, owned by Roma Wright-Smith, who went on to win fourteen CCs and the Hound Group at Crufts 1975. He was exported to Gary and Anna Kartsounis' Tula kennel in South Africa, where he finished top dog all breeds. He was flown to the World Show in Italy and won Best in Show.

The second dog to be bought in was Ch. Oakbark Armfield Joker, a Mintmaster son. He was out of Pat Jo Madam, a daughter of Storming's litter sister. Mintemaster was a Ligonier son, so the Meakins were picking up the strength of their original lines. Joker was mated to Newbold Sweet Martini, a bitch bought in from the Howarths. She was by Ch. Sun Courtier out of Ch. Oakbark Michaela. Out of this litter came Ch. Oakbark Mister Magic of Silkstone (owned by Roma Wright-Smith). Mister Magic then went on to sire three Champion sons: Ch. Gainscliff Renown (bred by Susie Williamson), Ch. Palmik Starsign (whose dam went back to Joker and Pyramid, bred by Mike Howgate), and Ch. Puddledock Swan Song (bred by Rachel Flatt).

As well as the two dogs bought in by Oakbark, the bitch, Flarepath Aquaria, was to play a very important part. When mated to Ch. Towercrest Flarepath Taurus (a Ligonier / Astri son), she produced the stunning fawn-and-white litter brother and sister, Champions Milord and Movie Queen. Movie Queen was mated to Joker to produce the dam of Ch. Oakbark Middleman (owned by Phil Moran Healy). Middleman's sire was Ch. Charmoll McTavish, again a dog carrying the Meakins' original bloodlines. She was then mated to Moonstorm of Oakbark – a son of Ch. Storming, and his dam was sister to the famous Ch. Dondelayo Roulette. Again, there was to come a brother and sister of influence – Oakbark Mister Blue and Ch. Oakbark Must Love.

When mated to Middleman, Must Love produced Ch. Oakbark Mary Rose. Oakbark Mister Blue did not gain his title, but he was a very influential sire. The kennel bought in two full brothers by Mister Blue, both of whom became Champions. They were Ch. Cottonmere Monty of Oakbark and Ch. Cottonmere Personality of Oakbark, bred by Miss D. Greenwood. Personality was exported to Frank Pieterse and Lee Benyon of the famous Statuesque Whippets in Australia, who had some years before imported Ch. Allgarth Envoy and the famous Ch. Donderlayo Statue (an Oakbark Pyramid grandson). Monty went on to win thirteen CCs with a Crufts Best of Breed, and again the kennel had bought in a dog that was to produce Champions.

Mrs Robinson's Savilepark Whippets are strongly bred to Monty. He is the sire of Ch. Master Shoemaker of Oakbark (who is out of the litter sister of Ch. O. Mary Rose), and out of Ch. Middleman's litter sister he produced Ch. Oakbark Generation Girl and World Ch. Oakbark Snow Queen. Generation Girl was top brood bitch in Britain 1992. Dennis said she is very much Number One girl at Oakbark. Mated to her half-brother, Ch. Master Shoemaker, she produced the full brothers, Ch. Oakbark Master Plan and Ch. Oakbark Mister Wonderful. When mated to Ch. Norwill Barley of Hammonds, the Muffinman son, she produced Oakbark Mozak (owned by the McLeods, Peperone).currently the winner of two CCs.

The Oakbark kennel has just made up its eighteenth Champion in Ch. Savilepark Saucy Shrimp of Oakbark, a daughter of Ch. Oakbark Master Plan. This kennel has done so much for Whippets, not only in Britain but worldwide. They have not only bred for themselves, they have always been willing to sell top-class Whippets to other exhibitors who have been able to found their own kennels on these famous lines. Eighteen Champions is a remarkable record – and with more CC winners waiting in the wings, there will be plenty more Champions to come.

NEVEDITH

The foundation of most top-kennels is a bitch, but for the Newtons, it was a dog puppy – bought for their daughter, Editha – who was to be the start of this famous line. Ch. Akeferry Jimmy, bred by Mr Pendleton, was sired by Cockrow Partridge of Crawshaw out of Eegee

Ch. Nevedith Paperweight: Winner of twelve CCs, Top Whippet 1984, and Top Whippet Stud Dog in 1985.

Jane – a combination of the two great stud forces, Ligonier and Tarragon. He had a brilliant show career, handled by Nev Newton, but as a stud dog he was to prove superb, siring ten English Champions and more overseas.

The Newtons were to buy in many lovely bitches by Jimmy, and their line started to build strength. Jimmy was mated to Ch. Skytime of Glenbervie (a double granddaughter of Ch. Cockrow Tarragon of Glenbervie) to produce Ch. Ruegeto Nina of Nevedith. Nina, in turn mated to Ch. Nevedith Bright Beret (a son of Akeferry Admiral, who was by Ch. Baydale Cinnamon out of a Tarragon daughter), produced Ch. Nevedith Hill Breeze. Another lovely Jimmy daughter campaigned by Nevedith, although owned by the Hills, was Ch. Crysbel Skylight of Nevedith, bred by Mary Crocker. Skylight was out of Ch. Crysbel Skylark, who was by Fleeting Fulmar, a son of Jimmy's litter sister. The next Champion bitch was Huntress of Nevedith (bred by Mr Kenny), a daughter of Ch. Harque to Huntsman out of Night Star of Nevedith. Huntress was a double great granddaughter of Jimmy.

The first top-winning son sired by Jimmy was Ch. Nut-Cracker of Nevedith, bred by Phil Moran Healy (Hillsdown). This dog was out of White Bud of Glenbervie, a granddaughter of Ch. Tarquogan: he gained his title quickly and was Best in Show at two Club Champion Shows before being exported to Italy. Jimmy also produced Champions for the following kennels: Pardee, Baydale, Mispickel, Sakonnet and Killigrew.

Ch. Nevedith Paperweight, a son of Nevedith Merry Monarch (by Jimmy out of Whitbarrow Mini Mist, who again went back to Cockrow and Glenbervie) proved to be a big winner. He won twelve CCs, Top Whippet in 1984, Top Whippet Stud Dog in 1985, and was the sire of the "Up" litter, which included: Portuguese, Spanish and International Ch. Nevedith Up at the Top, Am. Ch. Nevedith Up Sadaisy, and Eng. & Am. Ch. Nevedith Uptown Guy. Paperweight was exported to France in 1987 where he gained his title. On the way back from a show in Italy, his owner's car was stolen. The car was found abandoned and undamaged, but Paperweight and another Whippet had disappeared. Although substantial rewards were offered, there has never been any trace of the Whippets.

The "Up" litter were, again, out of a Jimmy daughter. Uptown Guy won three CCs and two BOBs, and both times was Reserve in the Hound Group. He was mated to Chilka Dairy Maid, owned by Mr and Mrs Barker, to produce the biggest winning Whippet of all time – Ch. Nutshell of Nevedith.

Nutshell has set a record that I am sure will never be surpassed. It includes: forty-four Challenge Certificates (thirty-seven with BOB), fifteen Reserve CCs, fifteen Hound Groups, eleven Reserve in Group, eight Best in Show All Breeds (General Championship Shows), five Reserve BIS, Top Dog All Breeds in 1989, Runner-up Top Dog All Breeds 1990 (losing by only one point), Hound Group and Reserve Best in Show at Crufts 1990, and winner of Pedigree Chum Champion Stakes Final 1991.

In December 1992 this lovely bitch whelped a litter to Ch. Pencloe Dutch Gold, and the resulting puppies proved to be outstanding. The dog, Nevedith Justa Jesta, won four Reserve CCs as a puppy, Justa Joy and Justa Jewel having won Best Puppy in breed at Championship Shows. Justa Jigsaw is now a Canadian Champion, and the star of the litter, Justa Jenie, has won two Challenge Certificates while still a minor puppy, and several Reserve CCs. She was Best Puppy in Show All Breeds at Darlington Ch. Show, Reserve Best Puppy in Show at the Hound Association Championship Show, qualified for the Pup of the Year final, and finished Top Whippet Puppy for 1993.

LOWGLEN

The Lowglen kennel of Fred Nicholas is another kennel which owed its great success to a dog. Ch. Lowglen Newbold Cavalier was the sire of nine English Champions. He was a very closely bred dog – his sire, Skydiver of Lowglen, was a son of Ch. Towercrest Flarepath Taurus, and his dam, Flarepath Caprice, was the result of a father and daughter mating between Ch. Ravensdowne Bright Star and Ch. Laguna Ravensdowne Astri. Cavalier was bred by Margery and Des Howarth, and he was the first Champion for Lowglen. Cavalier was also the sire of the first Champions for the Allgarths, the brother and sister, Envoy and Edelweiss (owned by Lowglen); and for Savile Park he produced the litter sisters, Ch. Sweet Harmony and Ch. Summer Season. I owned Summer Season in partnership with Freda Broadbent.

The kennel also added strength with the purchase of two more dogs, the offspring of which were to prove perfect mates for Cavalier. Lowglen Oakbark Masterminde from the Meakins, and the Masterminde son out of Ch. Laguna Ravensdowne Astri from the Woods, Ch. Flarepath Astrinought of Lowglen. The first Champion bred at Lowglen was Ch. Lowglen Cavalcade of Zarcrest (owned by the Boyles). He was a son of Cavalier out of a Masterminde daughter. Another Masterminde daughter, Lowglen Primadonna, was mated to Roger Stock's Dondelayo Repetition, a Tarragon Roulette son, to produce the lovely, quality pale-fawn Ch. Lowglen Holly Go Lightly. Primadonna's litter sister, Donna's Daydream, mated to Cavalier produced Byron Morgan's Ch. Ynysfor Aphrodite. The Astrinought Peppard Royal Mint daughter when mated to Cavalier produced Ch. Solera Scarlet Ribbons at Lowglen.

I have always much preferred showing dogs, and so I was pleased when yet three more

*Ch. Lowglen
Calvalcade of
Zarcrest and
his sister,
Cavalette,
sired by the
great Ch.
Lowglen
Newbold
Cavalier.*

males were introduced to the kennel. The first was Ch. Lowerdon Soldier Blue, bred by Sandra Marshall (by Cavalier out of the Oakbark Pyramid – Ch. Oakbark Michaela daughter, Newbold Startime). The second was Ch. Black Knight of Carmodian, a son of Ch. Baydale Cinnamon. Both Soldier Blue and Black Knight were owned in partnership with the Carmodian kennel of Mr and Mrs Carmichael. The third male to join the kennel was Ch. Novacroft Madrigal, owned in partnership with Freda Broadbent, bred by Dot Gardner.

The next Champion for the kennel was Ch. Lowglen Singing Bede. A double Cavalier granddaughter, she was by Ch. Soldier Blue out of Ch. Eidelweiss. When Ch. Singing Bede was mated to Madrigal, she produced Kath Sedgley's Ch. Lowglen Blue Mink at Dennydene. When mated to Ch. Carmodian Tawny Knight of Hutaka (a son of Ch. Black Knight out of Ch. Edelweiss's litter sister, Allgarth Countess Penelope) she produced the last Champion bred by Fred Nicholas, Ch. Lowglen Magic Moments.

Ch. Tawny Knight was to prove to be a very good sire and sired two top winners with strong Cavalier lines in their pedigrees. Ch. Sunsalve Hollidaze of Hutaka, bred by Terry Nethercott and owned by Anne Beckett–Bradshaw, was out of Lowglen Songbird (by Ch. Oakbark Middleman out of Ch. Lowglen Singing Bede). Hollidaze had a spectacular career, and out of only four Challenge Certificates, she won two Hound Groups, one Reserve BIS, and Best in Show at Bournemouth Championship Show. She was later exported to Sweden. The other top winner is Ch. Pennybeck Silver Sixpence, bred by the Jones and owned by Mr and Mrs Bird. Sixpence's dam, Pretty Ballerina of Pennybeck, is by Lowglen Cavalry Man, a Cavalier – Singing Bede son, He has won seven CCs and was the Hound Group winner at Three Counties Championship Show in 1992.

The fourth Champion by Tawny is the only one not to carry Cavalier on the dam's side, and he is the breed recordholder for dogs – Ch. Tilgreen Tornado – with twenty-five CCs to his name. He was bred by Mrs J.E. Smith and owned by Maureen Blanks. Another Cavalier daughter, Ch. Savile Park Sweet Harmony, was mated to Madrigal and produced Ch. Savile Park Subastral, for Barbara Robinson.

NIMRODEL

Mary Lowe founded her kennel in 1962 with the purchase of Willow of Allways (a daughter of Ch. Fieldspring Bartsia of Allway out of Ravensdowne Penelope) who was the dam of three Champions. The kennel is not only famous for its lovely, quality golden-fawns in the show ring, but it has also had many successes in the coursing field.

When Willow of Allways was mated to Miss Ironside's Ch. Poltesco Peewit, the first Champion for the kennel was produced – Ch. Nimrodel Willow Daughter. This bitch was also a Group and Reserve Best in Show winner at Birmingham National Championship Show. Peewit was also the sire of Ch. Nimrodel Ruff (his dam N. Wintersweet was by Mrs Cleeve's Ch. Dragonhill Woodpecker). Ruff went on to win many Challenge Certificates and was a top sire, siring six UK Champions. They were: Ch. Ringmore Riff Raff, Ch. Polteco Chough, Ch. Welstar Winning Dream, Ch. Wipstych Grandiflora, Ch. Woolsocks Summer Blaze, and Ch. Withaway Nimrodel.

Next came Ch. Nimrodel Wiveton, owned in partnership with Susan Baird. He was out of a Ruff daughter by Gwen Hemstock's Bartonia of Brough (who was by Ch. Iniskeller Lovely Silver, a son of Ch. Bartsia). Wiverton was also a Hound Group and Reserve Best in Show winner. He sired three Champions: the famous Ch. Welstar Royal Mint, Ch. Gainscliffe Chase the Ace (his dam was by Cavalier), and Ch. Mithrandir Gambit Dhahran,

Ch. Nimrodel Wanderer: Winner of twenty-two CCs, owned by June Minns. This dog is typical of the distinctive Nimrodel type, which has been so influential in the breed.

who was out of a granddaughter of Ruff. The top winner bred by Mary was Ch. Nimrodel Wanderer, owned by June Minns. He was sired by N. Dragoon (by Ruff, out of a daughter by Ch. Royal Mint).

Like his grandsire Mint, Wanderer was to win Challenge Certificates from the Veteran class. He had a great show record, winning twenty CCs, taking the male CC record from his grandsire, Mint, and he was also a Hound Group winner. He went on to sire three Champions: Ch. Baldrey Limited Edition of Juneric (owned by June Minns and bred by the Whites), Ch. Nimrodel Eagle Wings (owned by Mrs Turney) and Ch. Spyanfly Say No More, who achieved his title in 1993, and was Best in Show at the Hound Association Championship Show.

Over the years, the Nimrodel type never deviated, and with selective line breeding, Champions have been bred on to breed Champions. The Ruff daughter, Ch. W. Grandiflora, produced Hilda Meek and Mrs Griffiths' Ch. Nimrodel Rare Magic (by Ch. Royal Mint), and when mated to Ch. Potesco High Seas, she produced Ch. Nimrodel Peerless, whose litter brother, Pegasus, won the East Anglian Ch. Coursing Stakes three times. Mary has always had a great interest in blacks and blues. She bred her first black, Ch. N. Noir, out of the top coursing bitch, Nimrodel Djakanta, who was mated to the Ruff son Ch. Woolsocks Summer Blaze. There are also ten Nimrodel Champions overseas.

THE CURRENT SCENE

There are many up-and-coming breeders now establishing their own lines from stock from the highly influential kennels I have highlighted. There are also a number of very good Whippet breeders, who have been limited in the number of litters they have bred, but over the years they have had some very famous Whippets. We have had top breeders who have gone out of the breed for a few years due to business and family commitments, but they have never lost their interest in the Whippet, and, thankfully, we have some of them back again, breeding top-class Whippets.

SILKSTONE

A small kennel that has consistently shown and bred top-class Champion Whippets is Roma Wright-Smith (Silkstone). I know that Roma, when her family were young, much preferred to buy in a top-class puppy rather than breed a litter, but over the latter years she has been breeding a few litters and has produced some lovely Champion bitches. The success of this kennel has mainly come from the Oakbark lines, and latterly the Dondelayos.

The first Champion was Ch. Oakbark Merchant Prince who was a Hound Group winner. Unfortunately he was sterile, which was a great loss to the breed. Then came the famous Ch. Beeseeka Knight Errant of Silkstone. After a spectacular career, including winning the Hound Group at Crufts, he was exported to Gary and Anna Kartsounis in South Africa. The Meakins were to breed the next Champion in Ch. Oakbark Mister Magic of Silkstone.

The first bitch Champion for the kennel was the home-bred Ch. Silkstone Astella. She was by Oakbark Mr Blue out of Elmanash Saffron, a bitch carrying many lines back to Oakbark. After gaining her title she was also exported to South Africa. The next Champion bitch was

Ch. Silkstone Finesse: Successful in the show ring and as a brood bitch.

Diane Pearce.

Firedance of Silkstone – the last Champion to be bred by Anne Knight. Firedance was mated to Thurma Royal Reception (a completely Dondelayo-bred dog) and produced Ch. Silkstone Finesse. Both Firedance and Finesse qualified for the Pup of the Year finals. Both Finesse and Firedance were mated to Ch. Penelope Dutch Gold, and they produced excellent litters. Jewel in the Crown, a Finesse daughter, is the one that stayed at Silkstone. She was top Whippet puppy for 1992, won her title in 1993, and finished top winning Whippet for the year. She also won the Hound Group at Manchester Championship Show.

LOWERDON

The Lowerdon kennel of Sandra and Howard Marshall is another that owes much of its success to Oakbark lines. The Marshalls came into the breed in 1966 with a blue bitch of Ch. Mainly Allways breeding, bought for racing. This bitch was seen by Elsie Watson (Towercrest), who persuaded them to show her. At her first show she won three first prizes and the Marshalls were hooked on showing. The first CC for the kennel was won with Dixmoor Duberry (by Lowglen Oakbark Masterminde out of Dixmoor Dunfreda), bred by Dorothy Dicks. Dubarry was mated to Ch. Beeseeka Knight Errant at Silkstone and out of this litter came Kenyan Ch. Lowerden Sibella.

The Marshalls were then lucky enough to buy a young bitch, Newbold Startime (a Pyramid/Ch. Michaela daughter), bred by the Howarths. This bitch was to breed them two Champions. The first, sired by Ch. Lowglen Newbold Cavalier, was Ch. Lowerdon Soldier Blue, who won his first CC at ten months. She was then mated to Ch. Oakbark Middleman, and produced Ch. Lowerdon I Can Boogie. The star of the kennel was Ch. Jubilant Lady of Tygreen and Lowerdon, bred by Julie Smith, but the mating was planned by Roma Wright-Smith. Oakbark Miniver was mated to Ch. Beeseeka Knight Errant of Silkstone just before his departure to South Africa.

Jubilant Lady was to have a fabulous career. Molly Garrish (Fleeting) awarded her her first CC and Best of Breed at the City of Birmingham, she took the Hound Group under Reg

Ch. Jubilant Lady of Tygreen and Lowerdon winning the Hound Group at Crufts in 1979 under judge Molly Garrish (Fleeting).

Gadsden, and she took Best in Show under Maurice Gilliat. A week later she was to take her second CC under Anne Knight at Darlington, where she was BOB. She won the Group under Group Captain Sutton, and was Best in Show under Lionel Hamilton-Renwick. Like her sire, Knight Errant, she won the Group at Crufts, she was Best of Breed under Dorrie Anderson, and she won the Group under Mrs Garrish. She won a total of twelve CCs, two Reserve CCs, and also qualified for the Pedigree Chum Champions Stakes Finals and for the Veteran Stakes Finals.

She was mated to Oakbark Mister Blue and produced Swedish and Norwegian Ch. Lowerdon Dahlia. When mated to Ch. Oakbark Middleman, she produced Lowerdon Country Girl, who had a very successful puppy career, winning her Junior Warrant, but had to be retired due to injury. She was mated to Ch. Oakbark Muffinman and only produced two puppies, both bitches. They were Norwegian Ch. Lowerdon Masquerade and Int. Ch. Lowerdon Enchantress. Country Girl was mated again, this time to Lowerdon Never Say Die (a son of Ch. Master Shoemaker of Oakbark) and produced Lowerdon Sometimes A Lady, who to date has won one CC and three reserve CCs.

WELSTAR
Linda Jones of the Welstar Whippets, who does so much for Whippet Rescue, came into the breed in 1970. She bought a dog from the Rakinsons, Skyboat Silver Lining (a Mintmaster son out of Skyeboat Suntime of Glenbervie). He did very well for Linda, winning a Reserve CC. The foundation bitch of the kennel was Rasaday Amber, bred by Jill Chapman (a daughter of Mintmaster out of Oakbark Mirielle, a litter sister of Ch. Oakbark Michaela). Amber was to breed the first Champion for the kennel – the lovely Ch. Welstar Minted Model. Her sire was an outcross dog, Ch. Shalfleet Silver Knight of Skyeboat. Linda used this dog for his superb conformation and excellent movement.

Welstar Minted Model was mated to Ch. Nimrodel Wiverton (a son of Gwen Hemstock's

Bartonia of Brough), and out of this litter came the famous Ch. Welstar Royal Mint, owned by Gwen Hemstock. Mint held the dog CC record of nineteen CCs for two years, only to be beaten by his grandson, Nimrodel Wanderer, owned by June Minns. This record has just recently been beaten by Tilegreen Tornado. Mint was such a laster, and as a veteran he came out to win a further seven CCs and three Reserve CCs, which must be a record.

Minted Model mated to Ch. N. Ruff produced Ch. Welstar Winning Dream; and Mint mated back to Rasaday Amber produced Welstar Amber Royale, owned by the Mayers. W. Amber Royale produced two Champions for the Woolsocks kennel: Ch. Woolsocks Summer Blaze (by Ch. N. Ruff) and Morning Glory (by the Ruff grandson, Tweseldown Chevalier). Royal Mint produced two Champion bitches for Gwen Hemstock, out of Brough Genevieve (who was by Ch. Towercrest Flarepath Taurus out of Betonica of Brough, sister to Bartonia). The first was Ch. Brough Lady Devine, and a repeat mating produced Ch. Broughland Gina of Baldrey, the start of the Whites' Baldrey kennel.

BALDREY

The Whites were introduced to Gwen Hemstock at Crufts in 1980. Gwen had won the dog CC with Royal Mint; they enquired if she had any puppies for sale by Mint. There were two bitch puppies, and the Whites bought Ch. Gina unseen. She was their first Champion and their foundation bitch. Gina was mated to Ch. Shalfleet Silent Wish, and the Whites kept B. Silent Willow, who was the dam of Eric Minn's Ch. Baldrey Limited Edition of Juneric (by Ch. N. Wandererer).

The sire of Gina's next litter was Nimrodel Dragoon (a son of Ruff). Out of this litter came Ch. Baldrey Rainbow's End. She won three CCs, one Reserve CC, and a Hound Group. Her brother was Irish Ch. Baldrey Gold Blend, who won two Reserve CCs. A repeat mating produced B. Drogina (one CC), B. Drogeda (one CC and two Reserve CCs), and the dog, B. Drigorn, who also won well. Drigorn was mated to Silent Willow, and this was the first completely bred Baldrey litter. The dog from this litter, Baldrey Royal Crest, was mated to

Ch. Baldrey Limited Edition of Juneric: Winner of fifteen CCs.

Ch. B. Rainbow's End to produce the first totally home-bred Champion, Ch. Baldrey My Fair Lady. Baldrey Drogeda, owned by Linda Jones, was the dam of Ch. Welstar White Wine, who was sired by Ch. Woolsocks Summer Blaze.

BARMOLL

Molly McConkey has a very successful kennel, bred on mostly Shalfleet lines. Brandy Smash of Barmoll (who was by Selbrook Brandy of Shalfleet out of Spean Binnacle) was the start of today's Barmolls and was to breed Molly her first Champion. Mated to Garstones Nearco of Shalfleet, she produced Ch. Barmoll Beelzeebub, who was to prove to be a very good brood bitch. When Beelzeebub was mated to Ch. Samoems Silent Knight of Shalfleet, she produced the two sisters, B. Blue Lace and B. Banshee. Blue Lace mated to B. Bandwagon produced Canadian Ch. Barmoll Boy Drummer, owned by Mr Buchanan. Banshee was exported to the USA in 1982 and is behind many US Champions.

Ch. Beelzeebub's next litter was by Walkabout Wogans Brogue and produced B. Bewitched, Ch. Barmoll Beejapers, and the good sire, B. Bandwagon (two Reserve CCs). Beejapers went on to win four CCs and five Reserve CCs, and like Beelzeebub, she was to prove an excellent brood. Mated to Walkabout Wish Silently at Barmoll she produced the dog B. Bracken (two Reserve CCs), and the sisters B. Babycham of Timellie (two Reserve CCs), owned by Mrs Harms-Cooke, and Ch. Barmoll Beeswing at Walkabout, owned by Mrs S.A. Thompson but campaigned by June Minns – she won six CCs, five Reserve CCs, and was BOB at Crufts 1993. Molly kept Barmoll Breeze (one CC and one Reserve CC) and Ch. Barmoll Blaze of Gold (four CCs and six Reserve CCs).

Ch. Beejapers was then mated to Mary Rigby's black dog, Poachyn Pot Black, and produced the black Champion, Barmoll Blackthorn, owned by Mary Rigby. He took the dog CC at Crufts 1993, making it a Barmoll double. Following a repeat mating to Walkabout Wish Silently, Beejapers produced the Beaumonts' B. Beaujolais of Teisanlap (one CC and two Reserve CCs) and the white bitch presently being campaigned by Molly, Barmoll Bedazzled – a white bitch like her grandmother, Beelzeebub. Ch. Beejapers won top brood

Ch. Barmoll Beeswing at Walkabout: Best of Breed, Crufts 1993.

bitch in 1991 and 1993, and Walkabout Wish Silently of B. (a son of Ch. Shalfleet Silent Wish) was top sire in 989.

HILLSDOWN

Philip Moran-Healy owns this top kennel and has made up eight Champions, breeding seven of them. The exception was Ch. Oakbark Middleman, bought from the Meakins in 1980, who proved to be such a good sire. He was by Ch. Charmoll McTavish out of Oakbark Moving Picture.

The Hillsdown kennel success started with the two Glenbervie-bred bitches, White Bud of Glenbervie, and Denorsi Tinkermoon (although bred by Jack Peden, she was completely Glenbervie-bred). The first Champion for the kennel was Ch. Nutcracker of Nevedith (by Ch. Akeferry Jimmy out of White Bud), bought by the Newtons. Tinkermoon was mated to Ch. Charmoll McTavish and produced Ch. Hillsdown Tobique, and by a repeat mating she produced Ch. Hillsdown Repique. Repique was mated to his dam, Tinkermoon, to produce Ch. Hillsdown Roisin.

Ch. H. Tobique was mated to Ch. Black Knight of Carmodian, a son of Ch. Baydale Cinnamon who was by Ch. Charmoil McTavish. This combination produced the fabulous brood bitch Siobhan of Hillsdown. When mated to Ch. Oakbark Middleman, Siobhan produced the three outstanding brood bitches: Ch. Nicely Naughty at Birkonbrae (owned by Barbara Anderson), Moonbeam of Pencloe and Kienford (owned by Morag Bolton), and Hillsdown Mollie (owned by Jackie Bourdin in France). When Siobham was mated to Birkonbrae Coeur de Lyon (a son of Samarkand Sea Leopard and Ch. Nicely Naughty), she produced the outstanding sire Hillsdown Fergal.

Moonbeam of Pencloe and Kienford (who is a half-sister to Fergal) was mated to Fergal and produced the outstanding Ch. Pencloe Dutch Gold, winner of sixteen CCs and the first Whippet to go Best in Show at Crufts, 1992. After Crufts, Dutch was retired from competition. His first crop of puppies have been a great success, making him top Whippet Stud Dog for 1993.

Nicely Naughty was mated to Ch. Samarkand Beau-Ranger and produced Birkonbrae Buttons and Bows, a bitch who did a lot of top winning until breaking a leg. When mated to Fergal she produced the three sisters, Birkonbrae Everlasting Love (one CC, one Reserve CC, owned by Danny Gimour), Birkonbrae Forever Love (won a first at the only Ch. show to date, owned by Danielle Gilmour and Hayley Blacker), and Birkonbrae Summer Love in Sweden, who has been a top winner. Another dog bred at Hillsdown was Eng. Ir. Ch. Painted Pony, owned by Lucinda Thompson. He is by Shergar of Wildgen (a son of Middleman and Siobhan) out of Ch. Hillsdown Tobique. The latest Champion is Ch. Hillsdown Sorcerer (a son of Ch. Phinjani Pinball Wizard out of Hillsdown Blacque Rose, again a daughter of Siobhan).

PEPERONE

This successful kennel is owned by Jessie and Johnstone McCleod from Scotland. They came into Whippets in 1969 with a well-bred dog, Troutburn Silver Sabre (by Harvest Moon

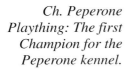

Ch. Peperone Plaything: The first Champion for the Peperone kennel.

of Glenbervie out of Cockrow Silver Dawn). He did a lot of winning at Championship and Open Shows, and was a racing Champion with the Whippet Club of Scotland for three years. The McCleods then purchased Skylark of Glenbervie from Arthur Nicholson. She was by Cockrow Woodchuck out of Ch. Sky Gypsy of Glenbervie, making her a double granddaughter of Ch. Cockrow Tarquogan of Glenbervie.

The first Peperone litter was bred in 1972 when Skylark was mated to Dondelayo Rufus of Oldwell. From this litter the bitch, Peperone Playgirl, was kept. She won four Reserve CCs before being exported to South Africa where she became a Champion. Skylark was next mated to Silver Sabre to produce the kennel's first Champion, Ch. Peperone Plaything. When Plaything was mated to Ch. Charmoll McTavish, a grandson of Tarquogan, she produced Ch. Peperone Papermate. A repeat mating produced the first male Champion for the kennel, Ch. Peperone Pepper. It was heartbreaking that this dog was sterile. A third mating resulted in only one surviving puppy, Peperone Papergirl.

In 1982 Hardknott Nectarine was bought in from Mrs Bennett. She was by Ch. Oakbark Middleman, the McTavish son, out of the lovely Ch. Belinda of Hardknott. She won two CCs and two Reserve CCs. Another Hardknott joined the kennel in 1986, Hardknott Quadrille. He was by Ch. Gainscliffe Renown out of the CC winning Hardknott Marietta, a daughter of Ch. Madrigal and Ch. Belinda. He won his title at sixteen months of age. He was mated to Papergirl and produced Ch. P. Peugot, top winning Whippet in Finland in 1990, and her brother, Passatt, owned by Jackie Crosby, winner of one CC and one Reserve CC. He is also the sire of Int. Ch. Play A While at Peperone, top winning Whippet in Sweden in 1989 and Top Stud Dog for 1993. Out of Peperone Promise (a daughter of H. Nectarine) he produced Ch. Dumbriton Wild About Harry, owned and bred by Danny Gilmour. Harry was exported to South Africa where he soon gained his title.

The latest Champion is Ch. Peperone Pink Gin (out of H. Nectarine by Peperone Playfair, a son of Madrigal and Papergirl), and her litter brother is Int. Ch. Peperone Pilsner, top Whippet male in Finland 1992-3. In 1992 Oakbark Mozak was purchased from the Meakins, and to date he has two CCs and one Reserve CC.

Ch. Mithrandir Spider Orchid: A top-winning bitch of the late eighties, early nineties.

MITHRANDIR

Pip Campbell bred another top winning bitch of the late eighties and early nineties – Ch. Mithrandir Spider Orchid – carrying very much the same lines as the Peperones. She is by Ch. Hardknott Mystery (a son of Madrigal and Belinda) out of Mithrandir Gavotte (who is by Hardknott Neptune of Mithrandir, litter brother to H. Nectarine, out of Peppermint of Peperone). Spider Orchid was mated to Ch. Pencloe Dutch Gold to produce Mithrandir Panning for Gold, who already has her Irish title plus two CCs to date. Her sister, M. Coin of the Realm, is a big winner for Dorianne Bernard in France.

FLAREPATH

It is lovely to have Irene and Harry Woods back in the ring again after a few years absence, due to their involvement with their horses. They will be remembered for owning or breeding such famous Champions as the lovely Ch. Laguna Ravensdowne Astri, a Best in Show

Ch. Ravensdowne Bright Star: A highly influential sire for the breed.

winner at General Championship shows, the top sire, Ch. Ravensdowne Bright Star, Ch. Towercrest Flarepath Taurus, another top sire, Ch. Flarepath Astrinomical, Ch. Flarepath Astrinought of Lowglen, Ch. Flarepath Tambilo Tarquin, and Ch. Gosemore Flarepath Auriga.

The new crop of Flarepaths are doing very well in the ring. Morning Sun at Flarepath, a daughter of Walkabout Wish Upon a Star, has two CCs, and the home-bred dog, Flarepath Eridon (by Ch. Gainscliffe Renown) was top Whippet puppy 1991 and has two CCs and two Reserve CCs. Waiting in the wings is the young Flarepath Rocket Man (by Ch. Phinjani Pinball Wizard out of Morning Sun).

COURTHILL

Roger Stock's Ch. Courthill Crown of Gold is currently making a name for herself in the show ring. She won her first CC at Darlington, her second at the Welsh Whippet Club Championship Show, and her third at LKA in 1993 – all her CCs have been with BOB. She is a daughter of Ch. Pencloe Dutch Gold out of Crown Affair of Courthill.

Due to business commitments, the Courthill kennel has not been in the show ring for quite a few years. Fortunately for Roger, his bitch line was kept for him by Barbara Wilton Clark. The first Champion for the kennel was Ch. Courthill Dondelayo Tiara, litter sister to Ch. D. Duette. Roger has had great success in combining the Dondelayo and Shalfleet lines that are

Ch. Courthill Crown of Gold: Currently making a name for herself in the show ring.

Irish Ch. Barnesmore Mercedes: A representative of the successful Irish kennel.

almost unrelated. The first home-bred Champion was Ch. Courthill Coronet (by Shalfeet the Bannerman, who was by Shalfleet Schelle) out of Shalfleet Spinning Top (her dam, Courthill Quadrille, was a daughter of Ch. Dondelayo Buckaroo out of Ch. Courthill Dondelayo Tiara). Tiara mated to Schelle produced Courthill Chorus Line, the dam of Ch. Shalfleet Showman of Courthill (his sire being Ch. Samoen's Silent Knight of Shalfleet). Showman had a very good career, and he won the Hound Group at the East of England Championship Show 1982. He was then exported to India. The Courthills have also produced many overseas Champions.

BARNESMORE

Margaret Martin's first Whippet was bought in 1974, mainly as a pet to replace a much-loved Saluki who had died. Sophie was rather too large for the show ring and so Margaret began to research which lines and type she preferred. From the outset she admired the Dondelayos for their classic type. She acquired a lovely monkey brindle bitch, Van Olreim Vanessa (who was by Dondelayo Lysander), and a brindle dog who became Irish Champion Town Crier of Lowerdon. From a mating of these two, she kept two bitches, both brindle – Barnesmore Lilac Wine and Irish Champion Barnesmore Lucy's Locket – and it is from these two bitches that all the present-day Barnesmores originate in an unbroken bitch line.

Lucinda Thompson, Margaret's sister, became involved with the kennel following the acquisition of Painted Pony from Phil Moran-Healy. This Whippet went on to gain his British and Irish titles, and then went on to have a profound influennce on all Lucinda's Whippets, stamping his type and soundness on his progeny. To date, the Barnesmore kennel has made up a total of seventeen Irish Champions.

Chapter Eleven

THE WHIPPET IN NORTH AMERICA

By HARRIET NASH LEE

The Whippet has been a companion of North Americans since the turn of the century. Much has been written in the past about the "roots" of the breed in the United States. Briefly, I will highlight some of the early breeders whose influence is still felt in present-day Whippets in the United States. It must be kept in mind that continental North America stretches some 3000 miles from coast to coast and 2500 miles from north to south. This may be one reason for the variety of type seen over this vast area. Today it is practicable to use a stud dog who lives 3000 miles away; in the past, however, this option was rather daunting.

EARLY BREEDERS

The first American Kennel Club (AKC) Champion in the United States was owned by the Bay View kennel. Owned by Karl Bjurman, this kennel was apparently a large one, housing other breeds as well. It certainly had some dogs imported from England, and from registrations it is noted that there was the Shirley bloodline in this kennel. The Bay View influence in Whippets was short-lived, however, and not in evidence after around 1912.

It is difficult to track the breed or kennels producing Whippets at this time, as many were shown and made up without being registered. In the late teens of the century Freeman Ford established the Arroyo kennel in California. Mr Ford was apparently quite taken with the Whippet and its athletic ability. With his kennel manager, James Young of Canada, Arroyo produced a line of both racing and show dogs. Many were imported from England and Canada. A black bitch, Ch. Sidlow Sloe Eyes of Arroyo (Tom Jack – Soakers Rose), an English import, can be found behind many American dogs today. It is interesting to note that Mr Young's daughter, Christine Cormany, is living in Las Vegas, Nevada and was one of the Grand Marshals for the 'Parade of Greats' at the 1994 AWC National Specialty held in Olympia, Washington. The Strathcona, Corsian and Strathoak kennel names are also seen behind many of today's dogs Meanwhile on the East Coast, Whippets were gaining in popularity. Some of the kennel names popular early on were Nomad, Freemanor, Bland's, Pocan, and Garden City, just to name a few.

MARDOMERE

Much has been written about Margaret Anderson's Mardomere kennel, and the Meander kennel, owned by the sisters, Judith and Julia Shearer. Both were highly successful, and must be rated as the dominant force in Whippets in the 1940s and 1950s.

Mrs Anderson's Mardomere kennel was a 'closed' kennel, as she did not have her dogs at stud to outside bitches and seldom sold puppies. With the aid of Percy Roberts, a professional handler who later became a very well-known all-breed judge in the US, Mrs Anderson imported several lovely dogs, including Ch. Flornell Glamorous (Tiptree Monk – Tiptree Christine). This bitch had a fabulous show career, including twenty-one Best in Shows and seventy Group wins. In one fifteen month period she went Best of Breed at fifty shows and was placed in forty-nine Groups!

Glamorous's litter brother, Ch. Tiptree Noel, was also imported by Mrs Anderson. Mrs Anderson allowed Noel to be bred to a Meander bitch, Ch. Frosty Morn of Meander (Ch. Mica of Meander – Meander Pickaninny), and this breeding produced Ch. Picardia Polkadot who was a consistent winner in the show ring in California. This bitch produced Ch. Picardia Fieldfare (Sunnysand O'Lazeland – Ch. Picardia Polkadot), who brought the Tiptree Noel line back to Meander kennel.

Probably one of the most memorable of the Mardomere imports, was the lovely Ch. Laguna Lucky Lad (Ch. Laguna Liege – Ch. Brekin Ballet Shoes). Apparently too big for success in the show ring in England, this exciting dog won handily in the United States and was the first Whippet to win the Hound Group at Westminster. Though never used at stud outside of Mardomere, he was the sire of eleven Champions.

Since Mrs Anderson ran a 'closed' kennel, there has, as one might expect, been a limited influence on the breed from her dogs. After her death, some of the Mardomere dogs were used by other kennels and did produce well. There was quite a rivalry between Mrs Anderson and the Shearer sisters. Both kennels were very successful in the show ring but seldom competed against one another.

MEANDER

While Mardomere was flourishing on Long Island, NY, in Virginia the Shearer sisters were busy maintaining the Meander kennel, which was already quite successful and well-known for their Whippets. Miss Judith and Miss Julia also raised race horses, Aberdeen Angus cattle and other breeds of dogs, notably the Pembroke Welsh Corgi and Foxhounds.

The Shearers imported heavily from England, and they succeeded in combining the lines they had imported (Tregear, Tiptree) with each other and with a Ch. Towyside Teasle daughter, Ch. Syndicate of Meander, to produce the 'Meander type'. Bo Bengtson described it so well when he said "Meander type usually signifies a solid red-fawn dog with dark pigmentation, quite tall by contemporary American standards and beautifully proportioned – a true 'Greyhound in miniature' without any of the stumpy, cut-off look or exaggerated toplines often seen elsewhere."

Because of their influence, the Shearer sisters controlled the American Whippet Club for years and set the standard for the breed. It is a well-known fact that Ch. Mica of Meander (Ch. Sandbrilliant of Meander – Ch. Syndicate of Meander) was the model for the American Whippet Breed Standard. He was not only a successful show dog but a great sire. (A beautiful bronze of this dog resides in the American Kennel Club Library.)

The Meander kennel had a tremendous influence on the breed, and breeders researching pedigrees today will usually find Meander dogs in their pedigrees. There is Meander behind several dogs in Europe currently, including the Bohem/ Whippoorwill, Autumn, Merci Isle and Paris imports; and of course the Badgewood line of Mrs Philip S.P. Fell goes back to Meander.

STONEY MEADOWS
In the 1940s Doris Wear was intrigued by the Whippet and purchased a family pet, Meander Topaz CD. From that beginning the well-known Stoney Meadows kennel developed and flourished. From her first litter out of Topaz, bred to Saddlerock Sho 'Deed' H Does, came Ch. Stoney Meadows Masquerade. He immediately put Stoney Meadows on the map by winning Best in Show, the breed at Westminster twice and placing in the Group both times, and winning Best of Breed at the American Whippet Club Specialty show twice.

One of the few able to acquire Mardomere breeding, Mrs Wear acquired Ch. Fashion of Mardomere (Ch. Tiptree Noel – Ch. Border Fly). Combining her Mander and Mardomere lines, she established a strong Stoney Meadows line that is behind many of the American kennels today. Stoney Meadows was certainly a dominant force on the East Coast during the 1960s and 1970s and well into the 1980s.

PENNYWORTH
This kennel, owned by Margaret Newcombe, was also a dominating presence in the 1950s and 1960s. Mrs Newcombe grew up in a 'doggy family' (her mother bred Chow Chows and won Best in Show at Westminster with a Sealyham Terrier), and she started in dogs by managing her mother's kennel and breeding Cocker Spaniels. As her maiden name was

Am. Ch. Willcare's Aged in Wood: Multiple Specialty and BIS winner. Winner of the Top Twenty competition in 1992. Bred by Margaret Newcombe and Paul Abraham. Owned by Claire Newcombe.

Penny, she registered her kennel name 'Pennyworth' in 1940. Shortly thereafter she fell in love with the Whippet. They happened to be Mardomere dogs, and Margaret Newcombe was able to purchase some of Margaret Anderson's stock. Her first home-bred Best in Show winner was Ch. Pennyworth Blue Iris (Ch. Impressive of Mardomere – Eng. Ch. Seagift Pennyworth). During the height of her kennel's influence on the breed, Margaret Newcombe imported many English dogs (in fact, she has had about a dozen English Champions) from the Seagift, Wingedfoot and Fleeting lines. Of these, Ch. Fleeting Falcon proved an excellent sire in the US and can be found in many pedigrees.

Of course Pennyworth is best known as being the home of Eng. Am. Ch. Courtenay Fleetfoot of Pennyworth. 'Ricky' to his friends, or 'the Golden One' as Margaret Newcombe often called him, set an incredible show record which has stood through many lovely dogs and is unlikely to be broken. He is the only Whippet to ever go Best in Show at Westminster. He retired the next year by winning the Group again. From February 1964 to February 1965, 'Ricky' was shown a total of thirty-six times, won Best in Show twenty-one times, thirty-two Hound Group Firsts, two Group Seconds, one Group Third, remaining undefeated in the breed every time except once. That was when Judith Shearer put him Best of Opposite Sex to Ch. Stoney Meadows Snow Queen (Stoney Meadows Epic – Ch. Snow Flurry of Meander). 'Ricky' proved a great sire, producing forty-five Champions, many from Falcon daughters. His best progeny came from breedings to Stoney Meadows bitches.

In 1966 Pennyworth imported Eng. Am. Ch. Tantivvey Diver of Pennyworth (Ch. Laguna Ligonier – Fleeting Fancy Free). Though Diver was not as successful in the show ring as Ricky, he certainly proved his worth as a sire. His best producing American son was Ch. Pennyworth Would You Believe, out of Ch. Pennyworth Burning Dream (Ricky – Stoney Meadows Snow Princess). 'Woody' was owned by Carol Willumsen of Willcare Whippets, and like his sire produced around twenty-five Champions.

Mrs Newcombe took a brief respite from Whippets, and the fancy was delighted to see her return to the ring with Ch. Bo-Betts Paddy Whack Dandy. She subsequently imported Eng. Am. Ch. Nevedith Uptown Guy, and has again become active in showing and breeding. Her daughter, Claire, is very active with her mother's breeding programme and has been showing a 'Woody' granddaughter, Ch. Willcare's Aged in Wood. This lovely bitch (also named Claire) was the 1992 Top Twenty winner, a multiple Best in Show winner, and Multiple Specialty winner. She has been in the top ten in Whippets for 1992, 1993 and 1994.

INFLUENTIAL IMPORTS
A number of Whippets have been imported and have had a major impact on Whippets in North America. They include: Ch. Charmoll Clansman, Ch. Dondelayo Buccaneer, Ch. Coveydown Greenbrae Wayfarer, Ch. Greenbrae Barn Dance, Ch. Ringmore Finisterre, Ch. Hardknott Maestro of Bohem, ROMX, Ch. Shalfleet Statesman, Ch. Whitbarrow Parsley, ROM, Aust. Can. Ch. Rothbury Replica, Eng. Am. Ch. Laguna Leisure, and Eng. Am. Ch. Ravenslodge Solitaire.

THE SIXTIES AND SEVENTIES
Ch. Greenbrae Barn Dance, the fine Ligonier son, imported by Mrs Clair Hodge of

*Ch. Hardknott Maestro
of Bohem ROMX.
Imported from the UK,
owned by Bo Bengtson.*

*Am. Ch. Misty Moor's Divine
Pleasure (Am. Ch. April's No
Fooling Around – Am. Ch.
Misty Moor's Ravendine
Alwyn): A grand-daughter of
Am. Ch. Misty Moor's
Chalmondoley, she is the all
time top producing American
Whippet bitch with twenty-one
Champions (from six litters) to
her credit.
Owned by Carol A. Harris.*

Highlights kennel, was a very prolific sire of the 1960s and still figures in many of today's leading bloodlines. His full brother, Ch. Coveydown Greenbrae Wayfarer, was imported to Canada by the Collings, and he has the distinction of having sired a bitch thought by many to be the greatest bitch of all times, Ch. Winterfold Bold Bid (Wayfarer – Stoney Meadows Bold Queen).

Bold Bid, better known as 'Hetty', was sold to Diane M. Bleeker (Morshor kennel) as Mrs Collings felt she should be campaigned and knew that Ms Bleeker would do that. She ultimately came to the Sporting Fields kennel of Mr and Mrs James E. Butt. Hetty was not only a great show dog but also a producer. She is the dam of several very important stud dogs, littermates Ch. Morshor's Bold N' Courageous (by a Barn Dance great-grandson) and Ch. Morshor's Appraxin Ariel. Bold N' Courageous sired the beautiful Ch. Gold Dust's Twenty Four Karat, winner of four AWC Specialties. Ariel is in a great many pedigrees today as the sire of Ch. Misty Moor's Chalmondoley.

In the 1970s the Barn Dance grandson, Ch. Misty Moor's Chalmondoley, better known as 'Chummy', was in his prime. His breeder, Jerry Edwards co-owned the dog with Roberta Russ (Misty Moor). Mr Edwards successfully campaigned Chummy to a multiple Best in Show and Specialty winning career. The dog was heavily used at stud by breeders all over the US and Canada for the elegence he seemed to produce in his progeny. Today he is still the top producing sire, with over one hundred Champions to his credit. His progeny include multiple Best in Show children and Specialty winners, most notably Ch. Runner's Creme de la Creme (dam of the great sire Ch. Delacreme de la Renta) and Ch. Plumcreek I Am, and the prolific Ch. Plumcreek Chimney Swift.

PRESENT-DAY KENNELS

The 1980s saw a number of very fine dogs who were garnering top honours all over the country and, as is to be expected, a number of different breeders impacting the breed.

One of the most visible of these dogs was Ch. Sporting Fields Clansman, bred by Richard Sufficool and Bruce Tague and owned by Mr and Mrs James E. Butt. This Ch. Charmoll Clansman son was handled through most of his career by Mr Robert Forsyth and amassed an enviable career of fifty-nine all breed Best in Show wins. In 1984 'Bouy', as he was known, topped off his career by winning the AWC Western Specialty from the Veterans class.

During this same period and in the same part of the country, multiple Best in Show Ch. Lady Blair of Whippoorwill ROM was also being shown. This bitch, known for her wonderful movement, was from the Whippoorwill kennel of Barbara Henderson, VMD.

Am. Ch. Lady Blair of Whippoorwill ROM: Multiple BIS winner, and dam of two all breed BIS winners and a Specialty BIS winner in her first litter. Bred and owned by Barbara Henderson.

Am. Ch. Delacreme Demoiselle (left) and Am. Ch. Whippoorwill Bohem Aria, owned by Bo Bengtson.

Though shown on a limited basis and compiling a very respectable show record, Lady Blair's 'finest hours' were in the whelping box. 'Pinkie', as she was called, was out of Ch. Whitbarrow Parsley ROM (Eng Imp.) by a Barn Dance grandson. In her first litter, sired by Ch. Misty Moor's Thornwood Dondi (a Barn Dance grandson) she produced two Best in Show winners, Ch. Whippoorwill Diamond and Ch. Whippoorwill Tanzanite (believed to be the oldest Whippet to go all-breed BIS), and AWC Specialty and multiple Group winner Ch. Whippoorwill Precious Gem ROMX

Gem, co-owned with Dee Berger (Unicorn), produced another wonderful litter sired by Ch. Hardknott Maestro of Bohem ROMX. From this litter, two bitches have produced Best in Show daughters. Ch. Whippoorwill Bohem Aria, herself a Specialty winner, produced Specialty and Best in Show winner Ch. Bohem Moonshine Lullaby (Ch. Bohem American Way – Aria). Ch. Whippoorwill Sonatina, bred to Multiple Specialty winner Ch. Delacreme de la Renta, produced the lovely multiple Best in Show and Specialty winner Ch. Bohem Delacreme Demoiselle.

Best in Show winner Am. Ch. Bohem Moonshine Lullaby. Owned by Bo Bengtson.

PLUM CREEK
In the Mid West the Plum Creek kennel of Linda Larson had two stud dogs who were consistently producing winners in the show ring and on the field – Ch. Plumcreek Chimney Swift (Ch. Misty Moor's Chalmondoley – Plumcreed Black Turnstone) and his son, Ch. Plumcreek Walk on Water (out of an Eng. Am. Ch. Laguna Leisure daughter). Walk on Water, better known as Rapid, has been a very popular stud, as he produces nice type and dogs who are keen on the lure.

RUNNER'S
On the West coast, the Runner's dogs of Isobel Stoffers were much in evidence. Ch. Runner's Our Own Charisma (Ch. Eyleland Double or Nothing – Ch. Tesuqye of Flying W), a wonderful show bitch, had produced Ch. Runner's He's the Continental (Ch. Misty Moor's Royal Huntsman – Charisma) who following in his dam's footsteps with his successful multiple Best in Show career. He produced Ch. Lasma Continental Divide (Continental – Ariami's Victory Sensation F.Ch.), continuing in the Best in Show family tradition.

SAXON SHORE
The Saxon Shore Whippets of Daniel Lockhart also made an impact on the breed during this period. Ch. Saxon Shore Amber Waves ROMX (Ch. Rolling's Victor – Ch. Rafina Rhianda of Kamara ROM), has proved an excellent sire with numerous Specialty winning progeny. Probably his most notable yet, who is also making his presence felt, is Ch. Delacreme de la Renta ROMX ('Jason' – Ch. Runner's Creme de la Creme ROM), bred by Mary Dukes and now co-owned with Doris Bandoian. 'Oscar' had a very fine show career, winning multiple Specialties, but his recognition has come from his stud career. One of his most successful offspring is the lovely Ch. Ringmaster's Gold Fever (Oscar – Ch. Gold Dust's Limited

Am. Ch. Saxon Shore Amber Waves ROMX (Am. Ch. Rolling's Viktor – Am. Ch. Rafina Rhianda): Number three all time Whippet sire in America.

Am. Ch. Delacreme de la Renta ROMX (Am. Ch. Saxon Shore Amber Waves ROMX – Am. Ch. Runner's Creme de la Creme): Multiple Specialty winner and a highly influential sire. Owned and bred by Mary Dukes.

Eidition ROM), bred by Paul and Sue Abraham and owned by Carey and Lori Lawrence.

'Quiche' is a beautiful bitch with fantastic ring presence. A multiple Specialty winner herself, she has produced littermates, Ch. Starline Reign On and Ch. Starline's Claim to Fame (Ch. Hamrya's Lucky Charm – Quiche), who have both been very dominant in the ring, and Reign as an active stud. Claim to Fame (Brie) was winner of the 1994 National Specialty.

Ch. Ringmaster's Gold Fever: A daughter of Ch. Delacreme de la Renta ROMX.   Bergman

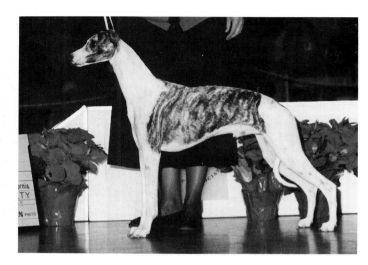

Am. Ch. Starline's Reign On: Successful in the show ring and now siring Champion offspring.

Rich Bergman.

SPORTING FIELD

On the East coast, the Sporting Fields kennel has already been mentioned. There always seems to be a contender from that kennel. The latest in a long line of successful dogs is Ch. Sporting Field's Kinsman (Ch. Sporting Field's Strider – Shilo's Avia of Sporting Fields). 'Luke' has been winning consistently since his puppyhood, and at this writing is the second top-winning Whippet of all time, close on the heels of his great-grandsire Ch. Sporting Field's Clansman, with fifty-four Best in Shows. He has been used heavily as a stud dog, and there are now many of his offspring in the ring carrying on his superb showmanship. Luke was winner of the Top Twenty competition held in conjunction with the National Specialty in 1994.

Am. Ch. Whippoorwill Tanager (Am. Ch. Whippetrees Raisin Cain – Am. Ch. Lady Blair of Whippoorwill ROM): Pictured at twelve years of age this dog has passed on his exceptional movement to his offspring.

Am. Can. Ch. Saxon Shore Flash Dance (Am. Can. Saxon Shore Amber Waves – Am. Ch. Rafina Patent Pending): Multiple Group and Specialty winner, dam of ten Champions.

BO-BETT

In the South, the Bo-Bett kennels of Carol Harris was producing a fine line of Whippets, and in 1989 had three dogs ranked in the Top Twenty: Ch. Bo-Bett's Snow Bunny, Ch. Bo-Bett's Starman of Carib and Ch. Bo-Bett's Wild Waylon. At the present, Ms Harris has cut back on her Whippet activities, though her dogs are still figuring in many of the winning pedigrees.

OTHER TOP KENNELS

There have been many breeders who have made consistent contributions with their breeding programmes in the last ten years. To name them all would be difficult and the likelihood of omission is great. The following are a few breeders and dogs, previously unmentioned, which this writer feels are impacting the Whippets in the US.

SURREY HILL: Carolyn Bowers' Whippets have certainly had an impact in many other kennels' programmes. Ch. Surrey Hill's Houston, F. Ch. (Whippoorwill Moonstone ROM – Ch. Allerei's Bolero ROM) can be found in many of the top winning dogs' pedigrees. His success as a stud led many to his sire, even though he was never shown due to a leg injury, and Houston in turn had a very successful stud career late in his life. (Moonstone was another of the incredible first litter of Lady Blair).

CHELSEA: The Chelsea kennel of Lee and Deanne Christianson has been breeding a fine line of Whippets, numbering many Specialty winners and two Best in Futurity winners. Ch. Drakkar of Oxford, F. Ch. (Moonstone – Ch. Chelsea Saffron ROM) is proving himself not only in the ring but as a stud.

KARASAR: The Karasar kennel of Kerri Kuper has also produced well with multiple Group winners and Top Twenty contenders.

Ch. Fenwick of Whippoorwill ROM: A dominant sire found in many of today's pedigrees.

Ch. and Am. Ch. Nevedith Uptown Guy, sire of Ch. Nutshell of Nevedith, the British breed record holder.

LEADING STUD DOGS

Mention must be made of several dogs who may be seen in many pedigrees today. These dogs have been successfully used by breeders across the country and will be seen for years to come in our Whippet pedigrees. There is no order of importance in their mention, as some are still active as studs and their full impact cannot be measured:

Ch. Elysain A-Few Perrier, F. Ch. (Ch. Plumcreek Walk on Water ROMX – Ch. A-Few Marthasville), a multiple Specialty winner and Top Twenty contender; Ch. Morshor's Majestic Dell ROMX (Ch. Plumcreek Walk on Water – Ch. Morshor's Royal Bid) and his son Ch. Morshor's Majestic Prince ROM (Dell – Ch. Morshor's Crown Jewel), both great showmen and dominant sires; Ch. Hamyra's Lucky Charm (M. Majestic Prince – Ch.

Hamrya's Moonscape v Tyobi), who unfortunately met an early untimely death, and his son, Ch. Broadstrider By George (Lucky Charm – Aymes N Raybar's Miss Oceana), who is currently a very popular stud. Ch. Fenwick of Whippoorwill ROM (a littermate of the great producing Lady Blair of Whippoorwill), who hated the show ring but can be found in the pedigrees of many of the successful dogs of today; Ch. Merci Isle Meridian (Oscar – Ch. Merci Isle Hot Flowers), a National Specialty winner in 1993, and his son Ch. Merci Isle Burncoat Babylon (Meridian – Ch. Morshor's Appraxin Sheree), the 1992 Futurity winner and a Specialty winner.

LEADING DAMS

Having mentioned dogs, it only seems fair to mention the bitches! It is more difficult to single out dams as they are not as prolific as the studs. Besides the bitches mentioned previously, here are a few of the bitches that come to mind: Ch. Roving Roulette, F. Ch (Ch. Swiftsure Happy Daze, F. Ch. ARM – Ch. Stoney Meadows Miss Julia), a National Specialty winner, Multiple Group winner and Best in Field winner; Ch. Prophecy's Promises Promises (Ch. Sihilo's Satisfaction Gar N'Teed – Morshor's Calyspo), a multiple Best in Show, Group winner and winner of the 1993 Top Twenty; Ch. Whitbarrow Parsley ROM (Eng. imp.), dam of Lady Blair and Fenwick – she produced rich colour and lovely substance; Ch. Allerie's Ain't Misbehavin', F. Ch. (Ch. Surrey Hill's Houston, F. Ch. ROMX – Allerei's Shaharizad F. Ch.), multiple Specialty winner and one of my favourites; Ch. Rafina Firlights Emily (Ch. Delacreme de la Renta ROMX – Ch. Rafina Bunny Hop), winner of the 1991 Top Twenty; Ch. Gold Dust's Limited Edition ROM (Ch. Stoney Meadows North Star ROM – Ch. Gold Dust Twenty Four Karat), a bitch who has consistently produced well; Ch. Misty Moor's Divine Pleasure ROMX (Ch. April's No Fooling Around – Ch. Misty Moor's Ravendune Alwyn) – Deveny is the top producing Whippet bitch of all times with more than twenty Champions to her credit.

Am. Can. Ch. Alerei's Aint Misbehavin F. Ch. ROM (Am. Can. Ch. Surrey Hills Houston F Ch. ROMX – Allerei Shaharizad F Ch.): Multiple Specialty and Group winner; dam of best in Show and Specialty winners.

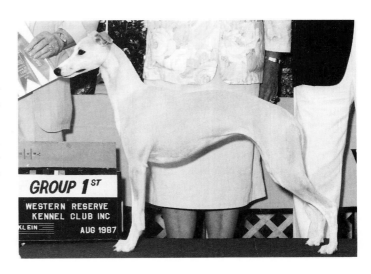

GROUP 1ST
WESTERN RESERVE
KENNEL CLUB INC
KLEIN   AUG 1987

CANADA

As in the US, Whippets have recently gained in popularity in Canada. However, though Canada is similar in width to the US, there does not seem to be as much breeding 'between the coasts'. Nevertheless, there are many fine dogs on both coasts. In 1993 the National Whippet Club of Canada was organised, and the first National Specialty was held in Calgary in July 1994. Formed by a group of dedicated Whippet fanciers, this club will now be guardian of the Whippet Standard in Canada.

INFLUENTIAL KENNELS

WOODSMOKE

Many breeders of Whippets in Canada began with stock from the Winterfold kennel of Martine Collings as their foundations – most notably, the Woodsmoke kennel of Pat Miller and the Alery kennel established by Allan Pepper and Terry Taft. Ms Miller is currently the top breeder of Whippets in Canada with Can. Am. Ch. Woodsmokes Share A Moment (Aust. Can. Ch. Rothbury Replica – Can. Am. Ch. Woodsmokes Wintermoon) as the top winning Canadian-bred Whippet of all time.

Replica (Eng. Aust. Ch. Dondelayo Statue – Andiamo Colomba) has sired well for Ms Miller, with Can. Ch. Woodsmokes All Ablaze (Replica – Woodsmokes Wait A Moment) following in his sire's footsteps. All Ablaze, owned by Wiebke Heron of Amazone Whippets, is the sire of the young bitch, Am. Ch. Woodsmokes Wrapped in Rainbows (All Ablaze – Am. Can. Ch. Antares Perlier), who was Best of Breed at Westminster 1994.

ALERY

Allan Pepper and Terry Taft's Alery kennel began with Winterfold Shining Hour as a foundation bitch. She produced the top Whippet in Canada for 1971, Ch. Alery White Warlock (Ch. Morshor's Whirlaway – Shining Hour). Warlock went on to sire Ch. Astrologer of Alery (Warlock – Lorribrook Fandango), winner of an American Whippet Club Specialty show and top Whippet in Canada in 1980. In 1982 Astrologer's son, Ch. Alery Astrologer's Antares, took top honours.

LORRICBROOK

Another dominant kennel has been Max Magder's Lorricbrook Whippets. Mr Magder imported Ch. Dondelayo Buccaneer (Ch. Dondelayo Buckaroo – Ch. Dondelayo Duette), who became a great show dog and successful stud with many Champion offspring including nine American champions. Mr Magder subsequently imported Can. Ch. Shalfleet Statesman (Eng. Ch. Samoems Silent Knight of Shalfleet – Eng. Ch. Courthill Coronet) who continued to produce well for Lorricbrook.

OF COURSE

On the West coast, the Of Course kennel of Bill and Margaret Turpin was quite influential in both the show ring and in racing. They bred the first bitch to win an Award of Racing Merit,

Am. Can. Ch. Woodsmoke Share a Moment (Can. Aust. Ch. Rothbury Replica – Can. Ch. Woodsmoke's Winter Moon): Canada's current top winning Whippet with seventeen All Breed BIS.

Ch. Rockabye Ember Of Course (Pennyworth Tumbleweed – Sonna Rockabye Baby), and through her get dominated the racing scene for a number of years.

SWIFTSURE
The Swiftsure kennel, owned by Linda Buchholz, has also been an influence in the race and show scene. Ms Buchholz imported Ch. Marial's King Arthur CD (Ch. Forest Slim Jim – Ch. Eyeland Paisley) from the US kennel of Doug and Mary Beth Arthur, well-known for their dual-purpose Whippets – and his son, Ch. Swiftsure Happy Daze, ARM F. Ch. (King Arthur – Can. Ch. Ringo's Sonny Daze Of Course, Am. Can. F. Ch), became one of the most titled Whippets in Canada and, as previously mentioned, Mrs Buchholz is showing Am. Can. Ch. Swiftsure Out of Africa (Happy Daze – Ch. Surrey Hill's Savannah, F. Ch.), who is co-owned with Karen Bowers Lee. He is making his mark as his sire did.

OTHER TOP KENNELS
There are many breeders in Canada who should be mentioned as producing fine Whippets and, as with the US Whippets, there is concern for omitting someone. To name a few: the Ashgrove kennel of Christine De Pierre; Denroc Whippets bred by Tuck Turner; Devonair of Heather Dansereau – known for their versatile dogs; Flytes kennel of Dr Janet Lalonde (who is known for her work in combating the atrocious 'puppy milling' of dogs; Baccaret, which is now the prefix for Terry Taft; Nasusa Whippets of Sue Badick and her daughter, Carla.

There are still dogs carrying the Boarley and Mispickle prefixes that are contributing to the breed, though these kennels have left Canada and I believe are now located in England.

Dave Markus and Rob Lindey have combined current Canadian and American lines successfully in the Aikerskaill Whippets.

Though the time of the large breeding kennels has past, both in the US and in Canada, it seems obvious that Whippet breeders in North America have successfully continued to produce quality dogs though breeding on a much smaller scale.

Chapter Twelve

THE WHIPPET WORLDWIDE

SCANDINAVIA

Imported stock has played a very important role on the Scandinavian Whippet scene. Breeders have been lucky to have imported the best stock from around the world, and they must have about the widest gene pool possible. Their future should be assured. Norway's top Whippet and top bitch all-breeds was bred in France by Jackie Bourdin. Finland's top Whippet and also an all-breeds winner is the American-bred Woodbrooks Autumn Terra Bella I'm Redee. This Whippet is by Am. Ch. Chelsea Drakkar of Oxford out of Am. Ch. Whipporwill Fanfare, a daughter of Hardknott Maestro Bohem, and the breeder is Mrs B. Huffman, USA. Helya Mamninen has also imported top winners from the Peperone kennel owned by the McLeods. The top Whippet male in Finland is Peperone Pillsner.

The Scandinavians were so lucky to have Bo Bengtsson! He was responsible for importing some very influential sires, including Ch. Laguna Locomite who was probably one of Sweden's top winning Whippets of all time, Int. Ch. Laguna Leader who sired twenty-five Scandinavian Champions, and Int. Ch. Badgewood Mark Twain. The most important import of the seventies was Ch. Fleeting Flamboyant. How wise of Molly Garrish to let Bo have this dog, as the English Whippet breeders did not see his potential as a sire. In his first year in Sweden he ended one of the top dogs of all breeds. Flamboyant revolutionized the breed in Sweden, and his type is still dominant in many of today's Swedish Whippets.

Magnus Hagstedt has also done a lot for the Swedish Whippet. He imported the very good sire, bred by Karen Mesavage in France, Int. Dan. Bel. Ger. & Swed. Ch. So Proudly We Hail De Sac a Malices, who went on to sire one of Sweden's top Whippets, Int. Ch. Airecot Waistcoat, bred by Nenne Rumsten and Petter Fodstad, who were responsible for Int. Ch. Statuesque Personalised, who was on loan from Australia.

LEADING WHIPPETS

CH. ACCENT'S AKELA
By Ch. Amiant out of Pappamos Carola, born 1978.
Bred by Monika Jonsson and owned and shown by Marianne Ekvall.
Akela was top Whippet in Sweden 1979, 1981 and 1983; in 1982 she was also top bitch. Akela won BIS at the Whippet Club, Sighthound Club and at the Kennel Club. She had

three incredible wins at the Whippet club show at Skokloster – in 1980, 1982, and 1984 – and in 1981 she was BOS. In 1983 she crowned her career by winning BIS at Skokloster Sighthound Show. Her breeding goes back to old Swedish lines and also to Ch. Fleeting Flamboyant and Ch. Laguna Leader. She is top winning Whippet in Sweden of all time.

CH. GARDSJONS LOVISA
By Ch. Cornwater Comet out of Ch. Gardsjons Charlott, born 1979.
Bred and owned by Chatarina Ostring.
Lovisa is one of the best brood bitches of all time, with several Champion children and mother of top Whippet 1985. She won a little herself when she was shown, but never reached the top as a show Whippet. She won BIS at a Whippet Club show when she was twelve years old! She is behind all of the successful Gardsjons Whippets winning today. Lovisa was top brood bitch 1986, 1987 and 1988. Her father is litter brother to the famous Ch. Jubilant Lady of Tygreen and Lowerdon. Her mother is heavily line-bred on Ch. Fleeting Flamboyant.

Ch. Gardjons Lovisa: A highly influential brood bitch.

CH. HOUGHTONHILL ORBIT
By Ch. Novacroft Madrigal out of Ch. Crysbel Skylight of Nevedith, born 1982.
Bred by Ray Hill and jointly owned by Margareta Martensson and Sam Parmback.
Orbit was top Whippet in Sweden 1986, and was top dog 1984. He has been a very influential stud dog, although I think that his bloodlines have been more successful in Norway when put to the Dondelayo-based lines. Orbit was top stud dog in Sweden 1985 and 1986. He won BIS at the Whippet Club show at Skokloster under Ann Knight in 1987. He is also a Group winner.

Ch. Houghtonhill Orbit: Top Whippet in Sweden in 1986, Top Stud Dog in 1985 and 1986.

CH. GARDSJONS SIGMUND

By Gardsjons Odskar out of Ch. Gardsjons Lovisa, born 1983.

Sigmund is one of the best coming from Chatarina Ostring's famous kennel, Gardsjons. He became top Whippet in Sweden in 1985 at only two years old, and was top dog in 1988. Although he only mated a handful of bitches before becoming sterile, he managed to become top stud dog in both 1989 and 1990. He won BOS 1985 and 1988 at the Sighthound Club at Skokloster. His mother's background is mentioned above, but his father goes back to Ch. Fleeting Flamboyant several times over. Sigmund is a Group winner.

CH. BOHEM CALLAS OF WHIPPOORWILL

By Ch. Proud Fox of Whippoorwill out of Ch. Whippoorwill Bohem Aria, born 1986.

Bred by Bo Bengtsson and Barbara Henderson. She is owned by Nenne Runsten, who handled her in the ring.

'Maria' was top Whippet in Sweden 1988. She did the 'double' at Skokloster, winning both BIS at the Whippet Club and then BIS the day after at the Sighthound Club. This was in 1988. She is the mother of top Whippet in Sweden 1991 and 1992, and was top brood bitch 1991. Her pedigree is special, as her father is a son of the famous British import to the USA, Ch. Greenbrae Barn Dance. Barn Dance is a son of Ch. Laguna Ligonier and a daughter of Ch. Greenbrae Laguna Lucia, so Maria is a unique connection to great old Whippets.

CH. STATUESQUE PERSONALISED

By Ch. Cottonmere Personality of Oakbark out of Ch. Statuesque Sundancer, born 1987.

'Person' was leased to Scandinavia from Australia by Nenne Runsten, but he was always shown by Nenne's husband, Petter Fodstad. He was bred by Frank and Lee Pieterse.

'Person' was top Whippet in Sweden 1990, and top stud dog 1991 and 1992. Like his kennelmate, Bohem Callas, he managed to win the 'double' at Skokloster in 1990. Although

Ch. Bohem Callas of Whippoorwill: A Best in Show winner, and a top brood bitch.

Ch. Statuesque Personalised: Top Whippet in Sweden in 1990, Top Stud Dog in 1991 and 1992.

an Australian import, his pedigree is completely English. His mother is by Ch. Allgarth Envoy out of Ch. Zipity Tartan Statuet (Tartan is by Ch. Dondelayo Statue out of Ch. Glenbervie Sky Belle). He now lives in Australia.

CH. PLAY A WHILE AT PEPERONE
By Ch. Hardknott Quadrille out of Mithrandir Gazelle, born 1987.
Bred by Mr and Mrs McLeod, owned and shown by Henrik Harling. 'Kim' was top Whippet in Sweden 1989 at only two years old. After that he has only been lightly shown

but was runner-up best Whippet in 1990 when 'Person' took honours. He became top stud dog in 1993 and is the dominant stud force at the moment. 'Kim' is line-bred on the beautiful Ch. Belinda of Hardknott. He is the father of two Skokloster winning children, and is also a Group winner.

CH. AIRSCOT WAISTCOAT
By Ch. So Proudly We Hail du Sac a Malices out of Ch. Bohem Callas of Whippoorwill, born 1989.
Bred by Nenne Runsten and Petter Fodstad; owned and shown by Ake Cronander.
'Petter' has been heavily shown and was the first Whippet to become top Whippet two years running, 1991 and 1992. In 1991 he went BIS at Skokloster at the Whippet Club show. He has started to have some winning children in the ring, but will surely be an asset with his interesting pedigree. 'Petter' is also a Group winner.

Ch. Airscot Waistcoat: Top Whippet in Sweden in 1991 and 1992.

Ch. Airscot Teenager: Top Whippet in Sweden in 1993.

CH. AIRSCOT TEENAGER
By Ch. Statuesque Personalised out of Airscot Waitrose (sister to Waistcoat), born 1990.
Bred and owned by Nenne Runsten; jointly shown by Nenne and Magnus Hagstedt.
'Tina' was campaigned last year and won nearly everything wherever she went. She won

BIS at the Whippet Club at Skokloster under Mrs McLeod, and became top Whippet 1993. She is a Group winner. She has just been retired from the ring to have a litter by Ch. Balzac Opsis Kalopsis (by Ch. Play a While at Peperone out of Ch. Marash Melody of Bayard). Opsis Kalopsis was last year's 'comet' among the dogs.

GERMANY

EARLY HISTORY

Whippets were first been registered in Germany as early as 1903, when a bitch called Fidel (Joli I ex Fidel I), born in 1899, found entry into the German Sighthound Stud Book. In those early days of the breed in Germany it was not uncommon for 'oversized' Italian Greyhounds to be shown and bred from as 'Whippets'. Before World War I quite a number of British Whippets were imported, most of them going back to Ch. Manorley Maori, and gradually Whippet type changed. For example, the imported dog Glenkoe Model (Ch. Manorley Maori ex Lady Graceful), born in 1911, is said to have been a near-perfect type who could still compete in the ring today. Knowing this, it seems strange that in following years emphasis was put on producing Whippets which did not show any features that were then attributed to Italian Greyhounds, such as elegance, sweeping lines, and 'class' in general.

Consequently, yet a different type of Whippet emerged, encouraged also by the wording in the German Breed Standard which, in several points, was divergent from the KC standard of the breed (this remained true up to the 1960s when the FCI Standard, an exact translation of the KC standard, came into play). From the 1920s onwards, track racing played a major part in German Whippet activities and Whippets are still judged with 'racing ability' in mind.

INFLUENTIAL IMPORTS

There were hardly any connections with Britain up to the 1950s, but then two extremely successful and influential dogs were imported. The first was Martyn of Allways (Ch. Sapperley Kinsman ex Bolney Starshine of Allways), who was the brother of Douglas Todd's celebrated Ch. Wingedfoot Marksman of Allways in England. Martyn not only finished his International Championship but also won the federal track-racing championship (Bundessiegerrennen) twice, thus proving once again that show-bred Whippets can, and do, run. The fact that he seems to have been almost totally overlooked as a stud dog (he sired eight litters in all, six for his owner!) is indicative for the situation of the breed in Germany. Among others, Martyn sired the famous brother and sister Chs. Famos and Fatme v. Schlesierland, bred by Martyn's owner, G. Barisch. The fawn/white-trimmed Fatme was possibly the most successful German-bred Whippet of all time, with numerous show and racing championships to her credit. Another import, Atom's Flash of Allways (Ch. Fieldspring Bartsia of Allways ex Ch. Red Atom) was an influential stud dog, mostly through his well-known son, Olaf v.d. Cloppenburg, who is behind many race winners.

LEADING BREEDERS

The Burgfried Whippets of Mrs von Watzdorf dominated the rings from the 1930s until well into the 1950s. She is probably the only German Whippet breeder who has ever judged the breed at an English Championship (Leicester 1956). Mrs Consbruch started her v.d. Kollau kennel in 1957. By combining old German and English breeding with Dutch racing blood, she has produced a long line of both ring and track winners up to the present day.

Mrs Kleineberg's v. Kleinen Berg kennel must rate as one of the most successful German Whippet kennels ever. She started off with a bitch of old German breeding in the late 1960s, but her younger winners are almost entirely based on Tim Teiller's famous Samoems strain. For a long time nearly all her dogs were solid reds with black masks, but she has now also incorporated some English and American blood (through Tim Teiller's Eng. Am. Can. Ch. Lorricbrook Runaway at Shalfleet, and his American bitch, Morshor Plumcreek Jasmine), and brightly coloured parti-colours carrying her affix can now be seen as well.

Another kennel worthy of mention is Mr and Mrs Senkbeil's Black Magic breeding establishment, which is almost entirely based on pure dual-purpose German breeding. Mrs Kiack's Superfly Whippets continue to be a successful combination of modern British and some French breeding. Mr and Mrs Kiack's English import, the almost all-white Int. Ch. Bredand Percy Vere (Ch. Gunsmith of Glenberrie ex Hillgarth Sunkist) was one of the most significant winners in the early 1980s.

The FlicFlac Whippets, owned by Thomas Munch, have made their mark on the scene since the second half of the 1980s. The kennel's foundation bitch, Ch. Fleetwing Opening Night, derives from Laguna, Dondelayo and Courthill imports into Switzerland. Among her descendants are the well-known fawn brother and sister, FlicFlac Angel Cake and Amazing Grace (by Ch. Samoem's Startin' Over), both multi-titled Champions – Angel Cake is also a top winning racer – plus the brindle/white brother and sister (by Eng. Am. Can. Ch. Lorricbrook Runaway at Shalfleet), FlicFlac Camelot and Chorus Line.

This kennel's English imports, carrying the Hammonds, Faracre, Courthill and Hillsdown prefixes, have all won extremely well. Int. Ger. KC Hammonds Simple Simon (Ch. Hammonds Sebastian ex Lydia of Hammonds by Hillsdown Fergal), bred by Angela Randall, must be considered one of the most successful British Whippets ever in Germany.

THE CURRENT SCENE

Whippets are not a popular breed in Germany. Bearing in mind that all puppies have to be registered, 175 registered Whippets (1992) is not a lot compared to the nation's population of 80 million people (neighbouring Switzerland with approximately 6 million inhabitants registers around 120 Whippets a year!).

For many years the German Sighthound Club (DWZRV) has been responsible for a strict size limit: dogs over 20ins and bitches over 18.75ins cannot be bred from, and judges apparently have been 'taught' that 'oversized' dogs must not win show awards either. Racing and, more recently, lure-coursing are still extremely popular among German Whippet owners, but while no-one doubts the benefits of these sporting activities, the fact remains that a different type of Whippet has been created over the years to meet the needs of the race track.

The newly formed Whippet Club Deutschland (WCD), thankfully, has no particular breeding/showing regulations. Enthusiastic club members have also managed to bring a whole string of famous British specialists over to judge their Breed Club shows in recent years – so there is still hope for the breed in Germany!

FRANCE

The Whippet has been a very popular breed in France since the middle of the nineteenth century. The French Whippet Club was formed in the late 1940s. The French have more stringent rules on size that most. However, many imports from England and America have left their mark. English bloodlines include Silkstone, Nevedith, Hillsdown, Mithrandir.

That clever breeder Karen Mesavage, of the Sac a Malices kennel, is by far the most international with her mix of English, American and French bloodlines, making an impact in Scandinavia and America. Jackie Bourdin is another breeder who has made a name for herself. Her imported bitch, Hillsdown Mollie, is the dam of many big winners including Norway's top Whippet, Int. Nor. Swed. Dan. Ch. Emotion du Manoir de la Grenouillere, owned by Espen Engh and Age Gjetnes. Jackie also had the best stud dog for five years running with Sandlena Astronomer, a son of Ch. Newbold Muffinman out of a granddaughter of Ch. Oakbark Michaela Oakbark Merry Maid.

Int. Ch. Nor. Swed. Dan. Ch. Emotion de Manoir de la Grenouillere: Top Bitch all breeds in Norway, 1992. Bred by Jackie Bourdin in France.

Claude Rebourg has had several English imports in her d'Escla kennel including the litter sister to the famous Ch. Jubilant Lady Of Tygreen and Lowerdon. The Lowerdon kennel of Sandra Marshall was also responsible for sending Ch. Hot Ice of Lowerdon and Ch. Lowerdon Enchantress to Claude. Chyton Notability, exported by Shirley Rawlings, has also done well. Ch. Neon of Nevedith, exported by the Newtons and owned by M. Cappi, has also proved to be a very useful sire.

HOLLAND

The Whippet show scene in Holland has been very much dominated by two or three top kennels. Tim Teiller's Samoems kennel has consistently produced top-class Whippets. His first imports were Wingedfoot, followed by Shalfleet, and he is another top breeder who has introduced American lines. Samoems Silent Knight of Shalfleet, imported by Barbara Wilton-Clark, was the first imported dog to become a British Champion. Tim Teiller's partner, Rene Matheewisen, has awarded Whippet Challenge Certificates in the UK.

The dam of Ch. Silent Knight, Shalfleet Sylvine, is behind another very successful kennel on the continent – the Sylvan Dwelling Whippets – owned by Lank Boa and Coos Huijsen. Frank Sampers imported very different bloodlines that were also highly successful. They included the Ch. Dondelayo Buckaroo son, Dondelayo Paint Tin, and Statesman of Silkstone, a son of Ch. Topall Newbold Miguel, a litter brother to the dam of Knight Errant. Statesman proved to be a very good sire and was used with great success in France and Germany.

OTHER EUROPEAN COUNTRIES

Italy is another country that has imported a string of English Champions. Baroness Renai della Rena imported Ch. Denhills Delectabelle after winning the CC at Crufts. The greatest number of imports were brought in by Maruo Carpone of the Almaglo kennel. He has owned many top dogs including the English Champions, Ch. Novacroft Starbright, Ch. Glenbervie White Frost, and Ch. Savilepark Sweet Harmony.

Switzerland and Austria have also imported top bloodlines through such Mrs Ranjt and Mrs Gut; they include Laguna, Courthill and Newbold.

Int. Ch. Savilepark Sweet Harmony (Ch. Lowglen Newbold Cavalier – Newbold Katrina), owned by Mauro Capone in Italy.

SOUTH AFRICA

EARLY HISTORY

Sadly enough, the earliest Whippets into this country are part of an unknown chapter.

However, KUSA records show that the first Whippet was registered in 1896. He was a dog called Beagle (sired by Will, dam unknown), registered on the November 10th 1896 by Jolly B. Adcock, registration number 1958. There were undoubtedly other Whippets in this country because we hear of their racing exploits, but when the Government banned dog racing it appears that the kennels of Whippets and Greyhounds were disbanded, and for all practical purposes, their dogs just vanished.

Mr and Mrs Peter Allen went to live in what was then Rhodesia, and they took Whippets with them from England. Lovely names like Fairly of Redmuir and Leprechaun of Greyworth appear enticingly in certain pedigrees, but there is no record of their previous owners. In the turbulence when Rhodesia became Zimbabwe, most of those who owned Whippets have also disappeared, and so early breed history remains an unanswered question.

INFLUENTIAL IMPORTS

Luckily for Whippet fanciers then and now, Anna Kartsounis arrived in South Africa in 1952, and she was to put Whippets on the map. After a disappointing start with four imported Whippets, Anna managed to buy a very famous Whippet, English Ch. Wingedfoot Clair de Lune, bred by Mr C. Douglass-Tood (by Ch. Wingedfoot Wild Goose ex Int. Ch. Wingedfoot Hildegarde). Clair, a stunning parti-colour, had won fourteen English CCs. Bo Bengtsson, Swedish and American breeder and judge, wrote of her "... one of the most admired English Whippets of all time, the gorgeous Ch. Wingedfoot Clair de Lune whose visual image I have forever tried to keep alive". Mrs D. McKay, in a weak moment, once described her as "the best Whippet she had ever seen".

In 1962 Clair arrived in whelp to Wingedfoot Indigo Imp, and became the foundation for the famous Tula kennel. The resultant litter of two dogs and three bitches formed the foundation of the current genetic base. Others imports to follow Clair included: Eng. Ch. Denorsi Moonduster of Glenbervie, who won his South African title with seventeen BISs, and sired a long row of Champions; Wingedfoot Susie Wong (Wingedfoot Golden Fleece ex Wingedfoot Georgina of Test) who arrived in February 1965; Wingedfoot Inadown Whispering Willow (Shalfleet Skyliner ex Inadown Whispering Witch) who arrived in July 1967, and Dondelayo Minette of Oldwell (Ch. Samarkands Greenbrae Tarragon ex Ch. Dondelayo Roulette) who arrived in June 1972.

October 1973 saw the arrival of sisters Glenbervie Sky Pink and Blue Sky, who were both out of Sky Gypsey of Glenbervie, a blue and white bitch, sired by Steel Bridge of Glenbervie. Eng. Ch. Denorsi Dancing Belle, bred by Jack Peden, arrived in May 1974. Belle was by Dondelayo Rufus of Oldwell ex Denorsi Tinkerbelle of Glenbervie. Mrs J. North-Row bred Barmaud Lord Halifax, a white and fawn parti, who arrived in October 1976. Halifax was by Eng. Ch. Flarepath Astrinought of Lowglen ex Nuzzle of Nevedith, who was litter sister to Nutcracker.

On January 25th 1977 the Kennel Club issued an export pedigree for Ch. Beseeka Knight Errant of Silkstone, who was bred by Mesdames M. Lamb and M. Hughes – and the Tula kennel acquired their most glamorous Whippet. Errant arrived fresh from winning the Group at Crufts, and he took the South African show world by storm, achieving his title

Ch. Beseeka Knight Errant of Silkstone winning Supreme Champion at the 1980 World Show.

very easily. In 1980 Anna and Gary took him to the World Show in Italy where he won through and made history by going Best in Show, gaining the title Supreme World Champion. 'Whiskey' as he was known, has sired many top winning sons and daughters, many of whom can be seen in the show ring today. Whiskey died in 1988 in the ownership of Anna Kartsounis' daughter.

June Pretorius helped to swell the quality of the genetic pool. She started by importing a lovely dog, Sticklepath Sailor Boy, who became a SA Champion in short order. Mrs Pretorius then brought in a bitch, Eng. Ch. Porthurst Martini Sweet. This was followed later by another import, this time from the famous Dondelayo kennel of Mrs Ann Knight, Dondelayo Hijack. Dondelayo Hijack preceded Dondelayo Tansy and Dondelayo Hijinx.

Neil Kay, in Natal, imported another top English line to the quality Whippets already here when he brought in Oakbark Mastermark of de Gratton. This proved to be a very successful decision, as the progeny has proved to be top-class. Not to be outdone by Transvaal imports, Rosemary Cabion in the Cape imported from another famous kennel, when she bought the bitch Harque to Yvette from Ann Argyle. Then Juliet Duthie brought in Shalfleet and Condicote Whippets from England.

WIDENING INFLUENCE
Interestingly enough, America has reaped the benefit of the Kartsounis Whippets. Christy Gordon-Creed started her Oldlands kennel in 1971 when she was living here in South Africa. When she moved back to her native USA she took her two Moonduster sons, who have since sired Champion stock in both North and South America. At the 1983 Specialty Show of the American Whippet Club in California, the winner was the fawn bitch Ch. Oldlands Singing in the Rain, a daughter of the imported Ch. Tula's Duststorm of Oldlands.

THE WHIPPET CLUB OF THE TRANSVAAL
Whippet owners in South Africa, like those in England prior to 1899, did not have a breed club of their own. There was no club to encourage a new generation of Whippet fanciers, no education on the breed, no-one to make representation to the South African Kennel Club (KUSA) or any show committee, which all seems rather strange when you consider the first Whippet registered with KUSA was in 1896. It was in 1983 that the idea of a South African club was first proposed by Jo Robertson (Merlanjo) and an augural meeting was held later that year. In 1984 The Whippet Club of the Transvaal was affiliated to the KUSA and from that time has grown in stature.

The first committee consisted of President, Jackie Jackson, Chairman, Joe Glaysher (Tanqueray Beagles), Vice Chair, Lota Rohmer, Secretary, Jo Robertson, and members Cyril Boardman, Ros Glaysher, Trevor and Elizabeth Hiscock, Merle McCullum and Peter and Rosemary Smith. The Club has steadily and strongly forged ahead, holding an Open Show yearly and gaining Championship status in 1990. The Club's first Championship Show was held in April 1991, with Editha Newton (Neverdith Whippets, UK) officiating, with over sixty Whippet entries. There is a yearly issue of a club magazine – *Whippet Whispers* – covering articles of interest to all hound owners. The Club gives helpful and instructive advice to followers of the breed, operates a Welfare and Rescue service, and keeps lists of approved Whippet judges.

AUSTRALIA
English imports have been a great influence on the Whippet scene in Australia. Not only have breeders imported very good Champion dogs, but these dogs have also been great producers. Int. Ch. Playmate of Allways was followed by such dogs as Lowglen Oakbark Masterminde, imported by the Martinique kennel owned by Terry Crawley and Ian Doherty. Masterminde was a very good sire in England, so it was not surprising that he was such an outstanding sire in his land of adoption. Terry and Ian later imported Ch. Solotown Simeon, a son of Ch. Oakbark Mister Magic of Silkstone out of a Knight Errant daughter – perfectly line-bred for Masterminde daughters.

Frank Pieterse and Lee Benyon were also responsible, along with Mr McCowage, for bringing to Australia such famous dogs as Ch. Allgarth Envoy, Ch. Dondelayo Statue and Ch. Cottonmere Personality of Oakbark. All these dogs were supremely bred and have all

Eng. Aust Ch. Dondelayo Statue: Imported from the UK to become a big influence on the Australian scene

had a great impact on the breed. How lucky the Australians are to have been able to import such great dogs! What was their gain must have surely been a great loss to the English Whippet.

Chapter Thirteen

THE COURSING WHIPPET

By GAY ROBERTSON

"Bred for speed and work" – the ultimate test of a Whippet as a representative of its breed is when it is matched against another of similar size and age on the coursing field. The reasons that owners go to considerable lengths to join Whippet coursing clubs and drive many miles to meetings vary from the ultra-competitive to those just wanting a pleasant day in the country with other Whippet enthusiasts. What brings them back again and again, win or lose and in all weathers, is the sheer thrill of seeing their dogs run.

Suddenly, the phrases of the Breed Standard coalesce into a living expression of "muscular power and strength with elegance and grace of outline" in a way that a Whippet trotting round a show ring can never convey. There is also the pleasure of seeing the happiness in the face of the Whippet who realises that a day's coursing is in store: the little cries of delight as the car draws up to the meeting, the greeting of friends, the wriggling anticipation, shrieks of excitement as the first hare gets up, the rush to the slipper as an old friend, tail-wagging as they stand or walk in slips, eagerly looking round for that first glimpse of a moving hare – and then, oh joy, they are slipped and they are off as fast as they can lay legs to the ground!

Whether it is a gruelling sixty seconds with first one Whippet then the other in the ascendant, or simply a long drawn out procession to the distant hedge, back they come, eyes shining, grinning from ear to ear, saying, this is life! If it is within their power, who can resist granting such pure joy.

ORGANISED COURSING

Whippet coursing, run under a strict set of rules, is a comparatively recent sport in Britain, starting in 1962 after some owners were offered a stake for Whippets at a combined Deerhound and Saluki meeting. Fired with enthusiasm, they decided to start a Whippet Coursing Club, with rules based on those of the National Coursing Club. These cover every aspect of the sport and were first drawn up by the Duke of Norfolk by order of Queen Elizabeth I in 1590. The National Coursing Club itself was not formed until 1858 when the huge proliferation of coursing clubs made a governing body, similar to the Jockey Club for racing, highly desirable.

The main problem facing the new Whippet Coursing Club was finding enough grounds on which to hold meetings to accommodate all the people who wanted to run their dogs. In

Slipper Bob Batch runs with the Whippets to get them balanced.

The relative sizes of hare and Whippet are clearly seen, Chyton Minstrel is not yet close enough to turn his quarry.

E. Walsh.

1971 two more clubs were formed, the East of England and the East Anglian Whippet Coursing Clubs, which prompted the formation of the National Whippet Coursing Club as a central body. This was marked by an Inter-Club meeting at the end of the 1972/3 season, which was so successful that a fourth club, the Woolley Whippet Coursing Club, was formed in the area near Huntingdon where the meeting had taken place. Today, the pressure on all clubs to take new members is intense, and all have succumbed to breaking the golden rule that twenty-five members is the maximum for whom a Whippet coursing club can hope to provide adequate sport.

THE ANTI-COURSING LOBBY

In writing about the enthusiasm of owners for coursing, no one can afford to ignore the fact that there is a body of organised opposition to the sport. The core of the argument of these organisations is that coursing is cruel to the hare. The Attlee Government set up a Royal Commission on Cruelty to Wild Animals (the Scott Henderson Committee) which reported in 1951 that coursing "involves no more suffering than the shooting of hares as ordinarily practised." Hares can do considerable damage to crops, and where they are not conserved for coursing, farmers shoot them by the hundred as a matter of routine.

Various Private Members' Bills were subsequently introduced, and these could have been successful, owing to MPs' apathy on the subject, without the tireless work of the late Lilah Shennan, then Chairman of the Standing Committee of the NCC. In 1975, the Labour Government introduced the Hare Coursing Bill, which led to more than a thousand people – among them many Whippet owners – turning up at Westminster on June 10th to lobby MPs against it. This was largely due to the efforts of the Coursing Supporters' Club formed by Anne and Sandy Mackenzie the previous year.

The Bill eventually sank on the dissolution of Parliament and when it was reintroduced in the House of Lords, Lord Denham persuaded the Government to set up a Select Committee to investigate the sport. This distinguished body attended Greyhound and Whippet coursing meetings, and considered oral and written evidence from all interested parties. A twenty-nine paragraph report

Madison Moonlake with the Whippet Coursing Club's Nicholl Cup, which he won outright after three successive victories. It was replaced with the Moonlake Cup.

was produced which concluded against the Bill on the grounds that it would not improve the welfare of hares, was impractical and against the natural laws of justice (the Bill sought only to abolish organized hare coursing).

That Bill did not proceed, and the next serious onslaught was the sweeping Wild Mammals (Protection) Bill in 1991, which sought to ban the chasing of all animals by all dogs – with a few specified exceptions. This was aimed primarily at hunting but had it succeeded, it would have criminalised any Whippet owner whose dog chased a rabbit on land he did not own, and enabled a court to disqualify him from owning dogs.

Referring to alleged public opinion that coursing should be abolished, the 1976 Select Committee pointed out "if those canvassed by societies are as ignorant of the facts as members of the Committee were before the inquiry, the value of the statement must be considered debatable."

THE FACTS

It is quite surprising that people who are well aware of unbalanced or inaccurate reporting of other subjects by the media, are prepared to believe everything they read or hear about coursing. So what are the facts?

1. Hares are *not* released from boxes on to ground from which there is no escape. Coursing on enclosed ground is already forbidden by law, and NCC rules forbid holding a meeting on ground on to which hares have been artificially moved and have not been at liberty for at least six months.
2. The object of coursing is *not* to catch hares but to compare the speed and ability of the two sighthounds on a points system. The overwhelming majority of courses do not end in a kill. When they do, one point may be awarded in exceptional circumstances.
3. The 1976 Select Committee rejected a common allegation that hunted hares suffer from intense stiffening of the limbs after an exhausting chase. Evidence was accepted from a professional zoologist and adviser to the RSPCA stating that any prey species which escapes from a predator will rapidly resume its normal activities. Nor does the hare suffer mentally since "it is biologically necessary that an animal of a prey species should not suffer psychologically by reason of being chased." (This statement is explained at some length.)

The committee estimated that of about 3000 hares coursed annually under NCC rules, twenty per cent were killed and of these, 120-150 were not killed instantly by dogs, but were taken from them and killed by specially appointed pickers-up in a time normally measured in seconds. On the rare occasions when the dogs carried the hare out of immediate reach, it was the opinion of the committee that in 75-80 per cent of the cases, the hare was already dead. These are not the figures of propaganda but the conclusions of a totally impartial Select Committee appointed to investigate the sport.

COURSING MEETINGS

The coursing season runs from September 14th to March 11th inclusive, but the preparation for a coursing meeting starts months in advance with applications to farmers for the use of land to course on. There are two kinds of coursing meeting:

Laguna Lively Lilt in full flight.

E. Walsh.

Laguna Lively Lilt demonstrating the need for strong loin and quarters in the double suspension gallop.

E. Walsh.

A WALKED MEETING in which the members and spectators walk in a line, preferably not more than 35 yards long, across ground where hares are thought to lie. When one gets up, the line halts while two Whippets are slipped and then once the course is over and the dogs have returned to their owners and been secured, the line continues.

A DRIVEN MEETING in which a line of beaters drives the hares towards a field designated as the running ground, and if they are skilful and the supply of hares plentiful, hares will appear within 30 to 60 yards of the pair of Whippets waiting to run, at regular intervals and not all at once.

COURSING STAKES

Advised by the Meeting Secretary as to how many hares they can expect to course on this particular ground, the Committee will decide what stakes to offer their members. A Whippet coursing stake is normally for eight Whippets, run on a knock-out system like a tennis tournament, so that the winning dog will have won three courses at the end of the day. Money prizes are a thing of the past but most clubs offer rosettes to winners and runners-up and sometimes there is a trophy to be won. These have more significance for owners than they do in the show world, possibly because there are no titles to be won.

While every stake is hotly contested – the overall standard nowadays is much higher than it was twenty years ago when a few good dogs dominated the sport – those of the Whippet Coursing Club are arguably the most prestigious because they are run at driven meetings where conditions are less chancy and more points are scored. A walked-up meeting may produce some thrilling courses, but the slips are unlikely to be consistently even and the "form" dog can easily be eliminated by pure bad luck.

The WCC main events are the Laguna and Moonlake (previously Nicholl) Cups for eight nominated bitches and dogs, and three height divisions: the Bannister, Foley Firecracker and Scrimgeour Cups. In addition, there is the Breeze of Ladiesfield Trophy, awarded by the committee to the most outstanding first or second year Whippet. The East of England runs the Autumn Trophy for dogs, the Franciscan Cup for bitches and a sixteen-dog Bob Blatch stake, confined to stake winners. The East Anglian Champion Stakes are sometimes run in dog and bitch divisions and sometimes mixed, but they also now have a qualifier; the Woolley Cup is mixed but they also have the Nijinsky dog cup and Ron Monk rosebowl for bitches. In addition, all clubs run very competitive veteran and puppy trophies.

RUNNING A STAKE

The details of the entry for each stake are printed on a card which also shows the names of the landowners and farmers over whose land the stakes are to be run, the stewards of the day and the Judge and Slipper. Directions to the meeting place will have been given on the entry form and cars and vans begin to arrive about 8am, although the actual meeting is not until 9am. Shortly before everyone moves to the first running field, either by car or on foot, the Secretary will announce which of the reserves are running in the stakes. Where (rarely) there are no available reserves, the dogs lacking opponents will run byes, which means that their owners can choose a dog to run with them and whatever happens in the course, the dog in the stake will be judged the winner and go through to the next round.

As the line is formed in the first field, the first pair of Whippets on the card are taken to the Slipper, a trained and licensed official – trained and licensed, because, under the rules of coursing, the hare must be given a start of at least 35 yards from Whippets (100 yards from Greyhounds) and leverets or unfit hares may not be coursed at all. The Slipper has only a few seconds to ascertain that the hare is suitable, that both dogs have seen it, get them balanced, into their stride and away together without giving one an advantage over the other.

The first dog on the card will be wearing a red knitted collar and will go to the Slipper's left; his opponent wears a white collar and goes to the right. They are buckled into slips – a specially constructed double collar yoked by a quick release mechanism that is activated by the Slipper pulling a cord. He then walks ahead of the line until a hare is spotted, and provided it is in sight of the dogs and not so distant that they would have no chance of reaching it before it disappeared, they are released and off they go. The Judge, also trained and licensed, follows on horseback, taking care not to impede either hare or dogs and awarding points for the value of the work done by each dog. It is necessary to understand these points in order to appreciate the merit of the win.

THE POINTS SYSTEM

SPEED: Up to 1 1/2 points are awarded for Speed, which is determined in the initial run-up to the hare.

THE GO-BYE is where a dog starts a clear length behind his opponent, passes him by a clear length and turns, or wrenches or trips or kills the hare. This earns 2 points or 3 if the dog is running on an outer circle.

THE TURN is where one dog is close enough to the hare to make her turn at least a right angle from the line she was taking and earns one point. If the hare turns of her own accord and the dogs merely follow her, no points are scored (except by the hare who will probably have increased her lead and diminished some of the dogs' stamina).

THE WRENCH is a turn of less than a right angle and worth half a point.

THE TRIP is where a dog makes an unsuccessful attempt to kill and the hare is thrown off her legs momentarily, or he snatches some fur without holding her and she runs on, worth one point.

THE KILL is worth up to one point if done with superior dash and skill, but may be without points if it happens through accidental circumstances or if the hare is turned to one dog by the other. The proportion of hares killed by Whippets is even lower than by Greyhounds and points are rarely scored.

Ch. Tweseldown Summer Chord and Summer Choir winning the brace class at the 1989 Ch. Hound Show. Consistently successful on the bench and in the field, the Tweseldowns exemplify the classic, line-bred Whippet.

A.V. Walker.

Laguna Black Larmite. Blacks and blues have done exceptionally well on the coursing field.

E. Walsh.

Most judges count the points by adding or subtracting them on the first colour to score. If a dog scores six points before his opponent scores anything, he starts scoring double until his opponent gets in. This is easier for Greyhounds to do than Whippets, since they can earn three points for the run-up. But in Whippet coursing, speed on the run-up is considered less important than the subsequent work. Many decisions have to be given on what is technically a no course since neither Whippet gets close enough to the hare to score, but the shortage of hares at a meeting means that a Slipper cannot afford to be choosy about a rather distant hare and some very long slips result.

Although coursing can be regarded as the supreme test of a Whippet, it is important to remember that the Judge is not there to decide which is the best dog, but which has scored the most points. Furthermore, he is looking at the course from a completely different angle from everyone else, being better placed than the spectators. In particular, he can see when the dogs are turning the hare and when they are merely following her.

He signals his decision by either taking a red handkerchief from his left pocket and waving it with his left hand or a white handkerchief from between the top two buttons of his coat, waved in his right hand. The Flag Steward raises the appropriate coloured flag for those who cannot see the Judge. This is the moment to mark the winner on your card, together with any comments that will help you recall the course later.

While all this has been going on, the next pair of Whippets should have been made ready in the slips. When all the dogs have run once, the first round winners run against each other in the next round in the same order, but they may be in different coloured collars. If 2, wearing white, beats 1 in the first round, he will be the top dog of the pair and therefore wear red against the winner of 3 and 4. If hares are plentiful, the Whippets may have barely returned from their previous course before the final comes round. In this case, they are allowed fifteen or twenty minutes rest (depending on the club) from the time the flag was raised on their previous course.

PHYSICAL ATTRIBUTES

The NWCC height limit for Whippets is twenty inches, which undoubtedly disqualifies the majority of show dogs in the ring today – but it has served the breed well. Originally introduced when most Whippet dogs and virtually all bitches were considerably less than twenty inches, it was intended to ensure a fair slip by limiting the disparity in size of the Whippets drawn against each other. A bitch under eighteen inches would be pulled off her feet by the neck, and have little chance of seeing the hare when walking or standing in slips with a dog three inches taller.

Today, there is an additional reason for maintaining the limit. As so many show dogs get taller and heavier, losing breed type and working ability simultaneously, the breeders dedicated to producing coursing dogs within the breed standard for size, type and conformation are keeping alive a gene pool of inestimable value to future generations. Judges may lament the passing of the "whippety" Whippet, but he is alive and well and using his hound instincts on the coursing field. It has to be said that there is an anomaly in allowing bitches up to twenty inches, since it becomes increasingly difficult to breed correct-sized dogs from such large stock. Although most of the new entry each year are bitches, nevertheless there are nearly always some good males too.

The other NWCC rule relating to runners is that they must be born during the year before the current season or earlier. Even at twelve months, most Whippets are not sufficiently mature to undergo the enormous strain on their growth plates, hearts and lungs from galloping after hares.

TOP COURSING WHIPPETS

While most pedigree Whippets will follow a hare with enthusiasm and verve, the competitively minded will note that some lines seem to do better than others. Results also depend on how extensively a particular Whippet is campaigned. With this in mind, I have asked owners of a number of successful dogs to nominate those dogs that, in their opinion, were the best, or gave them the most pleasure to watch.

LAGUNA

Pride of place must go to Mrs McKay and the Lagunas, for many years a top winning dual-purpose kennel and although regrettably no longer seen in the show ring, still a considerable force on the coursing field and the foundation of many successful lines. Ch. Laguna Ligonier both raced and coursed, and his grandson, Ch. Laguna Light Lagoon, was an enormously influential racing and coursing sire. One of Mrs McKay's particular favourites was Laguna Lilywhite who divided the Nicholl Cup with Laguna Lacquer, a Light Lagoon son, in 1971, and was the sire of Laguna Lauraine (WCR Ch. Candy), owned by Mrs Whittingham and one of the very few Whippets to excel at both racing and coursing. She in turn was the dam of Mrs Whittingham's great coursing bitch, the black Culverstreet Concubine, twice winner of the Laguna Cup and twenty other coursing stakes.

Although most people would associate Laguna with brindle particolours, nearly all the dogs regarded as particularly outstanding on the coursing field by Mrs McKay and her daughter, Mrs Bond Gunning, are black. Leezer and his sister, Leveret, were by Lacquer out

Chyton Bonne Chance winning the Laguna Cup at five years old. Many Whippets continue to course as veterans, long after their show careers would be finished. E. Walsh.

of Laguna Xmas Carol, and both inherited their sire's tendency to hunt around and help themselves to another hare unless they had had an exhausting course. In the early days, when hares were more plentiful and coursing was less competitive, Lacquer was notorious for holding up proceedings while he had just one more course and nobody held it against him, although those with dogs waiting in slips might get a little fraught. Nowadays, this is considered a heinous sin and can cause a dog to be banned by a club.

Leveret produced the seventeen-inch Laguna Black Lupina, who won a Puppy Cup and a number of stakes. Her brother, Leezer, was the sire of Leader, out of a Lilywhite daughter. From 1984/5 until 1991/2, Leader ran in 65 stakes, reaching 25 finals and winning a number of trophies, including the WCC Carswell Puppy Cup, Breeze of Ladiesfield Trophy, Bannister Trophy and the East of England WCC Autumn Trophy for dogs. He is specially precious to Mrs McKay, having been stolen from her kennels one night and recovered ten days later after an intensive local radio and press campaign caused the thieves to dump him on a road.

He is the sire of the black brindle particolour Laguna Lilt, twice winner of the Moonlake Cup and also of the Autumn Trophy – a remarkable achievement for a dog just over nineteen inches. Mrs Bond Gunning's personal favourite is the black Laguna Larmite (by Wyemere Black Casanova out of Laguna Black Lupina) who, she says, won three bitch cups out of sheer guts and determination.

TWESELDOWN

The Tweseldown Whippets have always been campaigned fearlessly on both bench and field. Chs. Winchat (Nimrodel Windhover ex Tweseldown Glentopic) and Summer Chord (Ch. Woolsocks Summer Blaze ex Tweseldown Royal Chortle) both ran well, with Chord's litter sister, Summer Choir, winning the Laguna cup before, tragically, both were killed on the road. Lady Anderson is held in such esteem and affection by the coursing fraternity that they commissioned a painting of Chord and presented it to her at Bournemouth Ch. Show in 1990.

Earlier favourites of Lady Anderson were one of a racing bred litter (Wilberswil Snowflake ex Silver Witch) she rescued and found homes for, save for the small, pale-fawn bitch who became Tweseldown Doublet, noted for not only killing the hare, but retrieving it as well. Tweseldown Lariat was a fast and doughty winner, in spite of having had a broken leg at three months which subsequently had to be re-broken and reset, leaving him with one leg turned permanently out.

Lariat was a grandsire of Miss Baird's Ch. Sound Barrier, winner of five CCs and five Reserve CCs, who was by Ch. Waycross Wishingstar ex Sunday Best. A totally honest dog who would run his heart out every time, he also had the ability to change his stride to suit the terrain which, in the opinion of his owner, led to his twice winning the Moonlake Cup when it was run over ridge and furrow at Great Coxwell. Ch. Sound Barrier was extensively used at stud and can be found in many of today's coursing pedigrees.

JIMANICA

Two sons who ran well for sisters Mrs Spencer-Thomas and Mrs Hill were Jimanica Jet Run and Jimanica Jungle Bunny, out of Katie Jubilee Lady of Jimanica. It is just as difficult to campaign littermates on the coursing field as it is in the ring, but Jet Run won the Moonlake and three other stakes, while Jungle Bunny also won four stakes (and his KCSB number) but ran into fewer finals. Other major winners in this partnership include Jazz Razmatazz of Jimanica (by Ch. Marshalls Milord of Faracre ex Kettleshill Enchantress) who has two Reserve CCs and is twice winner of the Laguna and runner-up for the Woolley Cup.

Ch. Sound Barrier with Jimanica Japonica produced Mr Mortimer's outstanding Jimanica Jaguar, winner of the Moonlake, the East of England Autumn Trophy and the Woolley Nijinsky Trophy for dogs. Jet Run is also a successful sire, notably of a Justcraina litter for Mrs Needs and of Mr and Mrs Barr's Banatay litter, who were all lucky enough to find coursing homes and dominated the 1992/3 season as puppies.

NIMRODEL

Mrs Lowe's Nimrodels were on the field from the early days of coursing. Chs. Ruff and Wiveton both ran well but she nominates Nimrodel Windleberry (Nimrodel Dragoon ex Nimrodel Wanton) as her best ever. She ran for only three seasons, her best performance being when she ran to the final of the Laguna.

Nimrodels who have coursed well in other hands include Col. Walsh's Nimrodel Ent Wife (Ch. Dragonhill Woodpecker ex Nimrodel Withywindle), a small, fawn bitch whose sole aim in life was to catch hares. In the 1973/4 season she ran twenty-one courses, losing three. Mr Hamilton's Nimrodel Bezique (WCR Ch. Chancerick Koh-i-Noor ex Nimrodel Belladonna) was a Laguna Cup winner, and Mrs Cox's Nimrodel Pegasus (Ch. Poltesco High Seas ex Ch. Wipstych Grandiflora) was for many years a top dog with the East Anglian club, running to nineteen finals of his thirty-nine stakes.

Four views of Jimanica Jet Run. Like his sire, Ch, Sound Barrier, he has been a top coursing sire for several seasons.

Photographs by Sally Anne Thompson.

Nimrodel Pegasus dominated East Anglian results for many years. Although Nimrodels are now rarely seen in the slips, they are behind many of today's winners.

Withaway Nimrodel being walked up.

E. Walsh

MARTINSELL

Another kennel that has fearlessly coursed show stock is Mrs Russell's and Mrs Brown's Martinsell. Although not numerous, they are always a force to be reckoned with, and the best in their view was Martinsell Sweet Alison (Ch. Shalfleet Silent Wish ex Martinsell Sweet Briar), a winner of the Firecracker. Ch Martinsell Grand Slam divided the first stake in which she ran, and then was killed in an accident. Sweet Alison was the dam of Martinsell Seaweed who ran brilliantly in Miss Shennon's ownership, winning the Autumn Dog Cup and running up in the Moonlake before he, too, had a fatal accident.

MOONLAKE

The Moonlakes stem from an outstanding dog of the seventies, Madishan Moonlake, who was a combination of Laguna and Allways lines. By Ch. Laguna Light Lagoon, he was one of a handful of pedigree dogs able to beat racing crossbreds and became a racing Champion, but his main achievement was in the coursing field. Running from 1971/2 to 1980/81, he was a finalist in twenty-five of his forty-four stakes, and one of only three Whippets in twenty years to achieve a success ratio of over fifty per cent (the others were Greywhip I'm Quickest and Chyton Bonne Chance). This was in spite of a crippling track injury which frequently caused him to be withdrawn mid-stake.

In 1979, a month short of his ninth birthday, he ran to the final of the Autumn Dog Cup, being withdrawn in favour of a grandson. His main claim to fame, however, is that after he had won the Nicholl Cup outright with three victories, it was replaced with the Moonlake Cup in his honour. Of his progeny, Mrs Ryan's Twiggen Waterwitch and Watergate divided the WCC Puppy Cup, and were Laguna and Moonlake Cup winners. Moonlake Miss Chiff (ex Nimrodel Chiff Chaff, a promising coursing bitch until she broke her leg) was under eighteen inches, but won half a dozen stakes. Mated to Ch. Deepridge Mintmaster, she produced two good winners, Moonlake Mint Sauce and Moonlake Master Copy of Chyton (CC and Reserve CC).

Mint Sauce did a hat-trick of puppy cups in his first season, and also won the Bannister and Moonlake Cups. His son, Moonlake Mickey Finn, was also the top coursing puppy of his year and won the Breeze of Ladiesfield and Bob Blatch trophies. Unfortunately, he became reluctant to return until he had found and coursed several hares each time he was slipped, which caused him to be banned by all three clubs with which he ran. Master Copy sired Ch. Chyton Copy-Press (four CCs, four Reserve CCs, and a Pedigree Chum Veteran Finalist) ex Sweet Briar, litter sister to Ch. Sound Barrier. Ch. Copy-Press won a puppy cup and the Moonlake, among other stakes, and also produced some prestigious winners for his owner-breeder Shirley Rawlings.

CHYTON

Like the Jimanicas and the Moonlakes, Mrs Rawlings' Chyton Whippets are expected to race, course and show, but her line from Maximilian of Chyton (Chancerick Kaspar ex Layer Albertine) is outstanding for its coursing success. Max, as he was known to everyone, was a major winner for five seasons, winning the Autumn Trophy three times and the

*Hungryhall Little
Luke, an early
winner of the Breeze
of Ladiesfield
Trophy, and a sire of
many good coursing
Whippets.*

Moonlake twice. His daughter, Chyton Bonne Chance (ex Bonnes Nouvelles de Chyton), has been a major winner every year since she started running in 1988/89, winning the Laguna twice, the Franciscan, the Foley Firecracker four times, and dividing the Bob Blatch with Chyton Minstrel (also by Maximilian of Chyton, ex Nimrodel Chantress of Chyton).

Another top winner by Maximilian is his breeder Mrs Dowsett's black Terichline Fidelius ex Haraiser Huntress. He is a multiple winner of the East of England and Woolley dog cups. He has also successfully bred on.

HUNGRYHALL
Joint founder of the East of England club (with Mrs MacDonald-Hall), the Hon. Mrs Richardson has had many outstanding coursing Whippets. Mrs Richardson's all-time favourite was Hungryhall Little Luke, a Breeze of Ladiesfield winning blue, who ran with great style as well as success, as did many of his progeny. Hungryhall Charity mated to Ch. Sound Barrier produced Hungryhall Hip Hip Hooray, winner and runner-up of the Moonlake; Hungryhall Bashful (Laguna Leader ex Sugar Candy) was twice winner of the Autumn Trophy.

CHEESEHOUSE
The first Whippet for Mrs MacDonald-Hall was a litter sister of Little Luke, Hungryhall Farthing. When mated to Laguna Blue Larne, she produced the seventeen-inch Cheesehouse Dime, a frequent winner against dogs much bigger than herself, and the first winner of the Franciscan Cup for Bitches. More recently, Mrs MacDonald-Hall's best have been litter sisters Cheesehouse Dollar (Moonlake Mint Sauce ex Yen of Cheesehouse), a Franciscan

winner, and Dinar, twice winner of the Scrimgeour. A third in this litter, Shekel, has won well for Mrs Nancy Matthews, breeder of their dam, whose bitches are consistently in the cards.

Chairman of the club, Mr Hamilton, considers his best-ever to be Jealous Hussy, by Laguna Larkin, noted as a sire of racing winners, from a daughter of Madishan Moonlake. Jealous Hussy was twice winner of both Laguna and Franciscan cups, plus the Bannister and other trophies. Mated to Maximilian of Chyton, she produced a major winner in June Honeymoon.

Chapter Fourteen

THE RACING WHIPPET

By GAY ROBERTSON

HISTORICAL BACKGROUND

Whippet racing was a recognised sport in Britain for nearly a hundred years before Greyhound racing was introduced in the 1920s. At its height, it was as popular as football until public support switched to the bigger dogs running in comfortable stadiums. Many people will be familiar with pictures of miners in cloth caps throwing their Whippets "to the rag", and with the probably apocryphal stories of Whippets fed on steak while the family starved on crusts of bread. Any Whippet worth keeping should have been able to keep itself and its owners well supplied with rabbit meat at least.

Although there were some tracks in the South, attempts to popularise the sport beyond the hard-core gamblers during the last century were not successful. Freeman Lloyd, whose book, *The Whippet and Race Dog* was published in 1894, worked tirelessly to promote Whippet racing for the gentry, writing about its suitability in *The Ladies' Home Journal*, and persuading his employers, the *Sporting Mirror*, to promote a Whippet Dog Handicap, which attracted 115 entries that year.

One owner, undeterred by the "pretty turbulent" scenes witnessed at other Whippet races, trained his dog, Flying Dutchman, with a bulldog named Evil Beast, who started halfway up the track to ensure a storming finish by the Whippet, who would presumably also be undeterred by possibly ferocious competitors, human or canine. Unfortunately, when it came to the race, Flying Dutchman, disconcerted by finding no Evil Beast at the halfway mark, stopped – for which he was renamed 'South Eastern Railway' by his disgruntled owner!

In 1899, Mr E.T. Cox's application to the Kennel Club for registration of the title of The Whippet Club was granted, and the following year the first Whippet Club Handicap was held at the Kennel Club show at Crystal Palace. Secretary of the club was Mr C. Smith, Mr Cox was clerk of the scales, Mr J.A. Tatham was recorded as handicapper, and the judge was Mr F.D. Mallett. To quote the *Kennel Gazette*: "The afternoon was beautifully fine, the track, a grass one, was as level as a billiard table, and the surroundings made it possible for everyone to see the racing without in any way interfering with the dogs. There was a total absence of any undesirable element, and altogether everything was as nice as it could be."

Sadly, there was also an almost total absence of entries, with just four sporting owners, the Duchess of Newcastle, president of the new club, Mrs Oughton Giles, chairman of the Ladies' Branch of the Kennel Club and a leading light in the Whippet Club, the secretary,

Mr Smith, and Mr Lamotte of the famous Shirley prefix, a well-known exhibitor. Between them, they made ten entries, but as that year seventy-four Whippets were registered with the Kennel Club, this was not a very good turnout. First prize of the Five Guinea Cup was won by Mrs Oughton Giles' Rosette of Radnage, who was also the second bitch in the breed to gain her show title. Second prize was won by the Duchess of Newcastle's Prince Barcaldine, and third was Mrs Oughton Giles' Mansfield Frivolity. There were a number of exhibitors among the spectators so subsequent events may have been better supported.

Sporting exhibitors certainly continued to race their show dogs – and over hurdles, too, as there is a mention in *Dog World* of Mrs Conway-Evans' Birthday Gift winning an important trial over hurdles at West Ham in 1929, beating a well-known London hurdler by five yards. Birthday Gift was much in demand as a stud dog and was the sire of Cloudy Morning, a very successful racing bitch owned by Mr Cyril Bugge, who also exhibited her, handled by Mr A. Trew.

At this time, Whippet racing came under the aegis of the English National Professional Sports Association, based in Manchester and constituted to be "composed of approved clubs, associations, and individuals interested in professional athletics or Whippet racing". Whether this was because Whippet racing was held at athletics stadiums or for some other reason, one can only guess, but events had to offer prize money of at least £5 to run under ENPSA rules and athletes and dogs had to be registered with similar details of past performance. The rules governing Whippet racing are much more detailed than those for athletics. Dogs over 36lbs were not permitted to run.

West Ham stadium ran Whippet races with a mechanical hare, under the rules of the London and South of England Centre of the ENPSA which were reported in the *Evening Standard* in the late 1920s. There could be as many as sixteen races in an evening with from six to nine dogs in a race. Cloudy Morning was a regular winner here, running the 300 yards in an average 22.32 seconds (time limit for the track was 23 seconds). The same owner's Rose Marie seems to have been decidedly faster, winning her race in 20.04 seconds, while Winston at 19.46 and Dick Turpin at 19.09 appear real flyers in comparison.

There is no record of whether races were scratch or handicap but the slower times were probably over hurdles, since Rose Marie was a Welsh champion hurdler before her London-based owner bought her. In 1927 the British Empire Whippet Club was formed "To promote the breeding of Whippets for Show and Racing", with the sporting Lord Lonsdale as its president. B.S. Fitter was vice-president and Captain W. Lewis Renwick chairman. Apart from the usual show objectives, the club aimed to ensure the provision of Whippet race track meetings, and a weekly club handicap was run on the Old Chingford track at Walthamstow.

THE POST-WAR YEARS

The Second World War curtailed dog activities all over the country and many kennels found it impossible to keep going. After the war, Whippet racing was first revived in the North with four clubs racing in 1945. The Potteries area had many enthusiasts for the old-style rag racing with dogs running down taped or netted lanes to their owners rather than following a mechanical lure, and this was the system used by the Stoke-on-Trent club in 1948. Up to

100 dogs could be expected at each meeting, and with bookmakers in attendance, races had to be run on handicap to preserve a gambling element and keep the interest of the hundreds of spectators. Since betting laws allowed only eight meetings a year in one field, the club had to "flap" from one area to another, hence the term flapping track.

The most sophisticated rag racing was run by the Furness Whippet Racing Club in Lancashire which acquired a betting licence in 1957, enabling it to construct a permanent track with electric traps and photo finish and floodlights. The introduction of betting tax in 1966 was a blow, but the club kept its licence until 1974. The surge of popularity of racing Whippets in the 1950s was met in the North West by crossing with Staffordshire bull terriers, according to Pauline Wilson, editor of *Whippet News,* and the broad chests and heads of some racing dogs would appear to support this theory. A more usual cross was with a small Greyhound, but as more and more clubs introduced height or weight limits, there was always the risk of puppies growing too big to race.

In 1967, the British Whippet Racing Association was formed "to promote greater friendship and understanding between the Whippet racing clubs" (some of whom had such intense rivalry that Whippets registered with one club were not allowed to run at events put on by its competitors and vice versa) "to give strength to the advancement of the sport...and to control and standardise Whippet racing." The Association was formed with ten autonomous regions but with clubs affiliated directly to the BWRA. Dogs have to be short-haired and Whippet-like in appearance and registered with an original name, i.e. one that has not been used before. National Championships for bend and straight racing are held each year and dogs must qualify to enter by coming first or second in their regional qualifying finals, usually held three weeks before. At the National Finals, the winners of each weight group are given the title Racing Champion by the BWRA, but as the dogs themselves are not pedigree dogs, this title is not recognized by the Kennel Club.

PEDIGREE RACING WHIPPETS

Pedigree Whippets have always been raced against cross-breds but only a handful have been able to compete on equal terms. During the 1960s a number of racing clubs in the South were running predominantly pedigree Whippets and members began to suggest that greyhound and other crosses should be excluded. At first, Kennel Club registration was required, which caused a problem for some owners whose Whippets were perfectly well bred but unregistered, so a judge or panel of judges was on hand to adjudicate on doubtful entries.

The Whippet Club, as senior breed club, felt that an organisation for pedigree Whippets similar to the BWRA would not only benefit the racing clubs who wanted to ensure that the Whippets racing with them were pure bred but would go some way to preventing a split in the breed between show and racing Whippets as had occurred in greyhounds. In consultation with the Kennel Club, the Whippet Club Racing Association was formed as a sub-committee of the Whippet Club and after some discussion – the club wanted the title Track Champion, the Kennel Club countered with Whippet Racing Champion – the title, Whippet Club Racing Champion, abbreviated to WCR Ch., was agreed.

The core of the WCRA is the passport system which operates to the benefit of a network of affiliated clubs. To run at a WCRA event, a Whippet must have a passport granted through the principal club with which they race. The secretary of the racing club will have already seen the pedigree and inoculation certificate of the Whippet before it begins its trials; once these are complete and the Whippet is accepted for racing, the secretary will supply a passport application form. This must be counter-signed by the breeder of the Whippet and a "seconder", who after checking the details against the dog adds a code indicating to the Registrar how certain they are that all details are correct – for example, that they know the breeder and the owner personally, may have seen the puppies in the nest and all names on the pedigree are known to them.

   If some breeding appears incorrect or is simply unknown to the seconder, they must indicate that further research is necessary. Kennel Club registration is required but is not taken as proof of pedigree as, regrettably, some unscrupulous breeders may try to infiltrate cross-bred stock either to win for themselves or to enhance their reputations. Five generations of "acceptable" breeding is therefore required for a passport. In addition, the Whippet must be at least twelve months old, weigh more than 14lbs and less than 30lbs and measure twenty-one inches or under at the shoulder. From 1996 this will be advanced to twenty inches in bitches. Markings showing everything from colours to scars and whether each toenail is light or dark are usually recorded by the club secretary or seconder on the passport which also has a colour photograph of the Whippet.

   Once a passport has been granted, the Whippet may enter the four WCRA Championship meetings held each year. Two of these are normally over 150 yards on the straight and two round bends of about 240 yards. When a Whippet wins the final of a championship weight group twice, it becomes a Whippet Club Racing Champion. Clubs affiliated to the WCRA are allowed to confine special events to holders of passports so that they can be sure that only pedigree Whippets compete.

THE TOP TEN

A points system to find the Top Ten pedigree racing Whippet dogs and bitches each year was proposed by Hilda Meek while she was serving on the WCRA committee and promoted in her very successful magazine, *Whippet Times* with the blessing of the WCRA in 1981. The magazine, which did so much to give racing people a voice in the breed and was of enormous benefit to the sport, is, alas, no more; but the event, now sponsored by a food additive manufacturer, is administered by a volunteer on the WCRA committee.

   Not all WCRA clubs take part in this competition, as some feel that the friendly, family atmosphere of Whippet racing is spoiled by the ultra-competitive who think only of winning points and titles and do nothing to support their home clubs, still less giving time to help novices in the sport. It has certainly concentrated breeders' minds on producing winners rather than the all-purpose Whippet and family pet for whom the club handicap races were devised.

BREEDING TO WIN

Ironically, the success of the WCRA, and the ever-increasing popularity of pedigree racing with various groups of people devising more leagues and unofficial titles, seems to have had

Cyril Bugge's Cloudy Morning by Mrs Conway-Evans' Birthday Gift. A regular racer at West Ham Stadium in the 1920s, she was also exhibited at shows. The straight stifle has always been regarded as a sign of speed by racing enthusiasts.

the opposite effect from that desired by the Whippet Club, since it is only in the last ten years that the breeding and conformation of the pedigree Whippets on the track have begun to diverge from those in the show ring. One reason is that show dogs are currently going through a phase where heavy bones leads to dogs considerably over the Standard in height, with substance to match. Whippets, by contrast, must weigh less than 30lbs to gain a racing passport, and the most common form of handicapping is on a "pound per yard" system, in which a 24lb Whippet starts four yards ahead of a 28lb dog, so the lighter-boned are favoured. Most regrettably, breeding only for speed and doubling up on some faults of conformation – like straight shoulders – has made them so prevalent as to be almost impossible to eradicate in some lines. On the plus side, temperaments are excellent: a Whippet that fights cannot race.

EARLY BLOODLINES

Nowadays, the received wisdom is that if you want a Whippet that will race successfully, you must obtain a puppy with racing parents, but this is taking a very narrow view and betrays an ignorance of the origins of the sport. The first Show Champion in the breed was owned by the Bottomley brothers, who dominated the show scene at the beginning of the century by picking up unknown stock at race tracks and re-registering them with their Manorley prefix, according to Bo Bengston in his book, *The Whippet.* The second dog Champion in the breed, Mr Vickers' Zuber, was born in 1889 and was by a racing dog, White Eye, said to run 200 yards in 12 seconds.

As we have seen, the first breed clubs ran racing handicaps patronized by exhibitors and when the WCRA was formed in 1970, current show prefixes were to be found throughout the racing entries and their breeding. Nor was it only one or two prefixes that proved successful. WCR Ch. Vangirl, dam of the best-ever pedigree racing bitch, Karyon Sootican Princess (WCR Ch. Picketty Witch), was by Shalfleet Saga and her female tail line went back to some famous Allways breeding, while Laguna, Ladiesfield, Rearsbylea, Russettwood, Boughton, Selbrook and Summersway were also commonplace in the pedigrees of winners. In 1979 the Whippet Club's 80th anniversary parade included two

Rosemarie: Welsh Champion hurdler. Coloured lines seem to do exceptionally well in both racing and coursing.

Karyon Sootican Princess (WCR Ch. Picketty Witch). The practice of awarding blue velvet coats, embroidered in gold, to the winners of major events, originated in the 1970s.

Whippets by Selbrook Brandy of Shalfleet: Barbara Wilton-Clark's Best in Show winner, Ch. Shalfleet Sequilla, and Mr and Mrs Birch's Sandspring Sir Edward, otherwise known as WCR Ch. Teddy Flash, top racing Whippet of the year.

PREDOMINANT STRAINS

A very influential litter was bred by Mrs Meek and her late partner, Mrs Griffith, from Chancerick Nimrodel Rosefinch, a litter sister to Ch. Nimrodel Ruff. Mated to Ebzan Noudini Bey-Noir, a son of Ch. Ladiesfield Bedazzled, she produced three racing champions, WCR Chs. Chancerick Kondor, Koh-i-Noor and Kala. Kondor went on to sire six racing Champions, Koh-i-Noor four, and Kala bred one in her only litter.

Since then two strains have predominated racing bloodlines due to the snowball effect of particular dogs being perceived as siring winners, and these two lines are to be found either separately or together in virtually all the winners of recent years. One is a Laguna line, chiefly through Laguna Larkin, a son of Ch. Laguna Light Lagoon, with some others going back directly to Light Lagoon. The second line goes to Ch. Ladiesfield Bedazzled, notably through the Chancerick K litter but also more recently through Kemerton Polo, a son of Bedazzled. In comparison with Whippets bred for show, coursing or as pets, the gene pool is dwindling as racing breeders flock to use the sires producing the fastest puppies. Size is always a consideration and dogs weighing less than 20lbs are popular. This has not resulted in a general diminution: most racing litters cover a wide spectrum of weights and heights.

PRIORITIES

Although they hope to maintain breed type, most racing breeders' main consideration is to breed speed to speed, and their second is for size. They may also look for an attractive head, but good ears are becoming hard to find. In spite of this preoccupation with speed, a glance at the times recorded in the passports of twenty years ago, shows that far from running faster, these modern racing Whippets are actually slower than the dogs at the back of their pedigrees. This is probably because the early racing dogs often came from show breeders who paid a lot of attention to conformation, and the show dogs of the day – not so large and heavy as they are now – had no difficulty in qualifying for a passport.

RACING NAMES

Few breeders of racing Whippets are interested in the lines behind their bitches, or have much knowledge of them. This can lead to unfortunate combinations of bloodlines that produce Whippets so untypical of the breed that rumours circulate suggesting that they must be cross-bred. In part this is due to the custom of Whippets racing not under their registered names but under made-up racing names that give no clue to the breeding. Thus the racegoer cannot unconsciously absorb the successful lines and kennels by seeing certain prefixes over and over again, building up a knowledge of the conformation of each dog in the pedigree in the way that successful show and coursing breeders do. If they are interested in a dog and ask for its pedigree, it is twice as difficult to make the connections between the names they read there and the siblings they have seen running.

UNITING THE BREED

In 1983, before the divergence became really apparent, the Whippet Club attempted to underline the "one breed" concept by offering classes confined to racing and coursing Whippets (separately) at the Members' Show in January. These are judged by breed experts who have personal experience of running their Whippets competitively and have the confidence of those lacking show experience. The classes are well filled, attracting some seventy exhibits. Although the coursing/show-bred dogs usually have the edge, some exceptionally free-moving racing dogs have successfully challenged for Best Racing/Coursing Exhibit. The next initiative by the Whippet Club to bridge the widening gap was to offer £100 to the owners of the first five Whippets to gain both titles in this country in the hope that dogs bred closely to the Breed Standard would be allowed to show their paces on the race track. If they were successful, and there is no reason why they should not be, they could prove extremely beneficial to the breed. So far, there have been no claimants.

LEADING WHIPPETS

Whippet racing is a sport where the newcomer frequently does well. Many racing champions are their owners' first Whippets, bought as pets, and this could be due to the very intense relationship most people have with their first Whippet: the one-to-one basis keeps each side finely tuned to the moods and desires of the other and, of course, the owner of a single Whippet has much more time to spend on it than someone who is spreading themselves between seven or eight.

WCR Ch. VANGIRL

This is well illustrated by the fortunes of WCR Ch. Vangirl who, after passing through various hands, none of whom could get her to race, was rescued at the age of fifteen months by Joyce Keable, now secretary of the very successful Andover club. Mrs Keable was living in an upstairs flat in Salisbury and the last thing she needed was a dog, particularly one so

At the starting traps: WCR Ch. Vangirl is in trap three.

nervous that a rabbit had chased it out of its run. It was November, and the bitch was also frightened of people, leaping into the canal when Mrs Keable took her out on their first evening together. Little by little, she improved, accompanying her owner to the school where she taught, until nine months later, she was racing – and racing well.

She won the first leg to her title at two years old, then had a setback when she was ripped by wire on holiday and took three days to come round from the subsequent anaesthetic. She was then mated to Abbotts Anny Pride (by Silver Belle of Auckland, a Ch. Playmate of Allways son, ex Blue Sovereign, grandparents of her dam) to produce Karyon Sootican Princess, the famous WCR Ch. Picketty Witch, winner of nine consecutive championships and ten in all for her owner, Terry Peart. Vangirl returned to racing and completed her champion title at the age of five. From her litter, Mrs Keable had retained a bitch, Karyon Solitaire (Woodpecker) who made life difficult by coming in season every four months but she produced Karyon Karayaka whose granddaughter, Karyon Goldies Fireflash, is dam of Mrs Keable's current lightweight racing champions, Firebug and Firepower. A repeat mating of Vangirl produced Karyon Shy Abbott (Canny Lad).

PICKETTY

Having had the enormous stroke of luck to acquire Picketty Witch, Mr Peart built on his success, mating her to the well-bred WCR Ch. Kondor, which gave him WCR Chs. Picketty Spook, Picketty Wizard and Picketty Witchdoctor, and then line breeding Spook back to

Karyon Shy Abbott, which produced WCR Ch. Picketty Magic, dam of the current WCR Ch. Picketty Midnight. Also in this litter was Mrs Keable's universally loved Lisa the Black Eared Bat, star correspondent of *Whippet Times* until her tragically early death. Wizard sired WCR Ch. Lord Spritely, a handsome particolour who was much admired when he put in an appearance at the Whippet Club show, playing outrageously to the gallery. The Pickettys now go back to Ch. Ladiesfield Bedazzled through the mating to Chancerick Kondor, although they are essentially line bred to Vangirl.

CASALOMA

Another consistently successful breeder since the early 1970s is Clare England, whose Casaloma Whippets feature in many a winning pedigree. As she only keeps bitches, her only racing champion is the black Casaloma Cassandra (WCR Ch. Beetle) out of a Selbrook bitch by a Summersway-bred dog, but Casaloma Misty Morn, Margaret Baker's WCR Ch. Sailor, bred on to produce WCR Ch. Casaloma Cobber. Mrs Baker was also successful with Casaloma Sea Pigeon (WCR Ch. Jolly): out of a bitch by Cobber, he was a son of Laguna Larkin (by Ch. Laguna Light Lagoon out of Mrs Whittingham's racing and coursing bitch, Laguna Lauraine/WCR Ch. Candy), who was a very popular racing sire bred to many different lines.

Mated to a daughter of Chancerick Kondor / WCR Ch. Nippy Girl, Jolly sired Jolly Nippy, for breeders Messrs Cairns who saw him gain his WCR Ch. title as Cousin Jack for his owner, and Pippawood Cardinal (WCR Ch. Tobermory Bay, a black dog out of the white and black Pippawood Painted Lady, who raced as Pebbledash until she broke her leg). Pippawood Cardinal, bred by Daphne Kitchen, is the sire of WCR Ch. Picketty Midnight. Other Jolly champions are Captain Poldark, Just Harlequin and Pebbles.

PIPPAWOOD

Laguna Larkin was also the sire of Mrs Kitchen's Kemerton Khaki (WCR Ch. Muffin), and this bitch, mated to a son of Ch. Ladiesfield Bedazzled, bred her the litter brothers Pippawood Mountain Apollo (WCR Ch. Always Skint) and Pippawood Marbled White (Slightly Dangerous) who between them accounted for many championship winners in the 1980s. Doubling up on Ch. Ladiesfield Bedazzled through Mountain Apollo and Kemerton Lauraine (WCR Ch. Pippa) produced Mrs Kitchen's most successful winner, Pippawood Spanish Festoon, owned and raced by Mr Rosser as WCR Ch. Zippa.

TELL UM STRAIGHT

Although Pippawood Mountain Apollo was the better racer, Mrs Kitchen considers Marbled White the overall better stud dog and he is the sire of Mrs Legg's Tell Um Straight (WCR Ch. Striker), bred by Mr and Mrs McDonald, out of Papedaro Camellia (On a Promise). A phenomenal racing dog, winning eight championships in three years, twenty-eight other titles and a further twenty-six Opens until injury cut short his career, Tell Um Straight looks set to break all records as a racing stud.

The litter also contained the 20lb Charlie's Pride (WCR Ch. Latchlifter), a popular stud dog, and a repeat mating produced WCR Chs. Little Minx and Powerful Paddy, a small

Tell Um Straight (WCR Ch. Striker) at full stretch. Typical of light-boned racing stock, he measures twenty inches at the shoulder and weighs in at 23lbs.   John Carson.

brindle particolour who is also becoming popular as a stud dog, since the retirement of Tell Um Straight, with reputedly one hundred racing progeny of which ten are already racing champions with more sure to follow. This breeding is dominating the results in the 1990s.

JOATER
Major and Mrs Coates are long-time and dedicated racing owners, starting with a bitch from Mrs Selby, Chinnor Oracle, by Curlands the Poacher. Taking expert advice, they mated her to Tarbuck of Heatherpard, a son of Ch. Laguna Light Lagoon, and were rewarded with their best-ever dog, Joater Misty (WCR Ch. White Wizard), who won 29 of his 41 Open races and five championships and was selected for the Personality Parade at Crufts in 1979 as the best pedigree racing Whippet. Mated to Casaloma Wren, litter sister to WCR Ch. Jolly, White Wizard produced Rob Doyle's WCR Ch. Hawkwind who in 1986 ran in four championships and twelve opens, reaching fifteen finals and winning eleven, with second place in two.

Joater Misty (WCR Ch. White Wizard) with owner-breeder Mrs Coates after parading at Crufts.

CARLSTREAM

Another Laguna-based line is Mrs Billingham's Carlstream prefix. Her Firebrace Quality Lady (WCR Ch. Silver Stream), a granddaughter of Selbrook Brandy of Shalfleet, is behind a line of racing champions starting with a litter to Tarbuck of Heatherpard which produced three: the bitches Silver Dream and Sierra and Mr Fuller's dog, Binfield Rocket. A subsequent litter to Laguna Larkin included Carlstream Fire Star, Mr Fuller's WCR Ch. Binfield Bullet, who, mated to Papedaro Clematis (WCR Ch. Platignum), produced WCR Chs. Binfield Jet and Freeman. Papedaro Clematis is litter sister to the dam of Tell Um Straight; they were bred by Mr and Mrs Spokes, to whom much of the credit for the early success of the WCRA belongs.

This colour line includes both Laguna and Ladiesfield lines through Mr Rees' WCR Ch. Jack's Boy, a grandson of Ch. Laguna Light Lagoon and one of the best racing dogs of the 1970s, and through another good racing sire, Swepstone Gem, a grandson of Rearsbylea Black Tarquin who was by Ladiesfield Black Magic. It also includes Blue Streak of Ocklynge, another good dog of the 1970s and sire of Miss Fisher's WCR Ch. Wirrawon Saucy Sylph. Wirrawons were racing long before the formation of the WCRA but Miss

Fisher tapped in to the Pippawood Mountain Apollo line to breed Wirrawon Saucy Slogan (WCR Ch. Melrose Sprite) from a daughter of Sylph.

Of the five racing Champions produced by Jack's Boy, four were in the litter bred by Mrs Richardson from Ricardo Roulette. Two were bought in by Mr Rees, who felt that WCR Ch. Our Kid would have proved even better than Jack's Boy had he not broken a leg early in life. Terry and Sue Ward, known throughout the racing world as suppliers of everything a Whippet could possibly need, started in 1971 with a bitch who became WCR Ch. Lucky Venture, by Russettwood Pageant, an influential early sire, out of the very fast Valhay Red Spinner. Mated to Jack's Boy, she bred them Happy Venture, the dam of WCR Chs. Beautiful Venture and Mississippi Venture by Swepstone Gem.

INJURIES

Although reference has been made to broken legs and other injuries, these have rarely occurred on race tracks, since all clubs take a great deal of trouble to make racing as safe as possible. The most common danger – and the one that is easiest to avoid – is racing puppies too young. Although Whippets *look* adult at ten months, skeletal maturity is not achieved until about fourteen months of age. In the hurly-burly of a race, a knock can injure the long, developing bones, especially the sensitive growth plates, which, in turn, can lead to deformities in the bone and even chronic lameness. Failure to recognise such lameness in the young dog, or failure to rest a puppy for a sufficient recovery period, can seriously jeopardise a racing career.

LURE COURSING

Lure coursing – or lure chasing as it should more properly be known, since the sighthounds are chasing the lure and cannot cause it to change direction – is a new sport in Britain, and offers a lot of fun without the pressure of a competitive event. It is run by the British Sighthound Field Association for all sighthounds, with meetings held at different venues round the country once a month from Spring to Autumn. Hounds run only against their own breed and must be at least a year old.

THE MEETING

The day before a meeting, members of the committee lay out the course, which is a continuous 500 metre round with bends and turns to simulate the running of a hare. Hounds start arriving at 9.0 a.m. and check in with the secretary who allocates them numbers. The owners are allowed to choose their opponents and decide whether to muzzle their dogs. No 'clearing' trials are necessary, but the owners may be warned off if the judges think their dogs are a danger to others.

The two judges, usually owners of different breeds, take their places on a raised platform from where they can see the entire course, with a score sheet for each runner. Maximum points are 25 for agility, 15 for enthusiasm, 15 for "follow", 20 for endurance and 25 for speed. However, speaking from experience, you might as well mark on a score of 1 to 5 for general ability and a genuine attempt to follow the lure, as, with such diversity of performance, it is impossible to mark consistently between, for example, 21 and 23 for agility, for one breed, let alone eight or nine. Even the most awkwardly galloping Whippet is going to appear more agile than a Wolfhound, and unless you have a close association with every breed, it is impossible to set a norm.

In America, where there are hundreds of lure meetings where judges can be trained, it is possible for them to become licensed to judge one breed at a time but in this country, with only a few meetings each year and for all breeds, novice judges can only learn by scoring all breeds on the day.

The best way to view the day's result is as a balance of two probably quite divergent opinions and regard the top twenty-five per cent as equally the best, the bottom twenty-five per cent as equally the least adept, and the rest as average performers who had neither the good or bad luck to attract the attention of the judges. In short, no one should take the scores seriously while the sport is in its infancy.

The first two owners take their hounds to the starting point and hand their numbers to a runner to give to the judges. The Hunt Master, standing at the start, having made sure that the lure operator and the judges are ready, asks the handlers "Are you ready?", and this is the actual beginning of the course. As the lure goes past and ahead of them, he will shout "Tally-Ho" and on the T the dogs should be slipped. If an owner slips before the T, a pre-slip penalty is incurred.

As in racing, the lure is most commonly a white plastic bag so that it will not become heavy on wet grass. It is not unknown for Whippets to get burn marks from the line but by and large, injuries are not common and the sport is not nearly so dangerous to the hounds as might be thought. One of the reasons for this is probably the lack of competitive pressure – and long may it continue that way! At the moment, the sport offers a decent, quite taxing gallop on a varied course which makes the Whippets use every part of their bodies and which they thoroughly enjoy. There are no winners or losers of individual courses which means that you can enjoy a friendly match against someone else's dog in which each owner can be convinced that their dog is performing better. Many of the hounds do run electrifyingly well and are very exciting to watch. In addition, there is the chance to meet people in other sighthound breeds in a relaxed, informal atmosphere and to learn more about all the breeds, including one's own, by watching them move at speed.

In the afternoon, the lure is reversed and everyone gets a second run in the other direction. If all has gone well, there may be time for multiple trials, running three or four hounds at once. It is lovely to see Whippets running in this way, but they should be muzzled to avoid a fight. The thrill of the chase can go to their heads like wine and the normal family hierarchy be up-ended as the young and fit race past their seniors, who may wish to reaffirm their status at the end. It is fascinating to see the different styles in which they run, which seem to reflect their characters. The Whippets that do best at lure coursing are those who lack top speed or the intelligence to anticipate the direction of the lure but doggedly pursue it with great enthusiasm and determination.

PREPARING YOUR WHIPPET
When you go lure coursing for the first time, do make sure that your Whippet is fit enough

to gallop five hundred yards on undulating ground, and if your dog is blowing hard at the finish, do not run him again in the afternoon. Give your Whippet some daily road walking to improve stamina, so the dog will be able to enjoy a full day's sport the next time. Keep your Whippet securely on a lead of adequate strength: there is an instant £10 fine for a loose dog, but worse than that, a fatal accident could be caused.

Red and white racing jackets are provided, but as they have to fit Afghans, Basenjis, Deerhounds and other dissimilar breeds, it is really better to have your own, as the majority are on the large size for Whippets. It is also really essential to have your own muzzle to be sure of a good fit.

As well as the sporting owners usually found on coursing fields and race tracks, lure coursing attracts quite a few well-known show breeders. The Astrophels, Barmolls and Shoalingams can be found at many of the venues, while Hammonds, Harque, Millwold and Boarley have featured at Belper. It is to be hoped that this excellent organisation will continue to attract the support it needs from all the sighthound breeds.

LURE COURSING IN THE USA

By William Dean Wright

THE SPORTS'S PIONEER

Lyle Gillette had a dream in 1964 of sighthounds utilising the abilities bred into them for centuries to pursue and capture game. These abilities would be preserved and a title would be awarded to sighthounds, who achieve a certain level of accomplishment, by the American Kennel Club. Lyle, a Borzoi breader and exhibitor in confirmation ring, lived in California. He, with the help of Borzoi and other sighthound owners, started the Open Field Coursing Association. The rules for this sport were written by Lyle using the American Kennel Club Beagle Trial Rules and Regulations as guidelines for this newly created activity. Although his main interest was Borzois, Lyle included additional sighthound breeds based on his correspondence with the American Kennel Club. This sport grew rapidly in California and spread to Colorado. Since hunting game without firearms was determined to be illegal in most states, this sport never spread to the East Coast.

In 1970 Lyle split away from that original organisation, due to unsafe conditions for the hounds. Hounds chasing a hare could not always stay in one field only, and a lot of the show dogs were becoming injured while attempting to go through barbed-wire fencing. After this split with the Open Field Coursing Association, Lyle spent all of his spare time talking to people to try to determine a plan for articicial coursing. He wanted a system that would offer a lure operator the ability to control the direction and speed of the lure and therefore the hounds, and one that could be adopted by all other areas of the country.

GAINING RECOGNITION

In 1972, in California, Lyle formed the American Sighthound Field Association, composed the rules for the sport and began holding trials. The new sport was a great success, spreading quickly to Colorado and Arizona in 1973, and by 1974 trials were being held for sighthounds on the East Coast of the United States. All of these trials were governed by the rules that had originated in California. Lyle wrote to the American Kennel Club regularly requesting the adoption of this sport as an ADC programme. He visited the American Kennel Club offices in New York on two separate occasions, and in 1978 the American Kennel Club sent a representative to the American Sighthound Field Association Annual Convention of Delegates meeting. The ADC has had a representative at every ASFA Convention since that year.

The ADC and ASFA had held several meetings to iron out a mutually acceptable programme of Lure Coursing, but could not work out all the differences in order to get the proposal approved by the ASFA Annual Convention of Delegates. In 1991 the American Kennel Club, with input into their programme from coursing sources, inaugurated their own programme of lure coursing. Lyle Gillette was the first person contacted to be told that his dream was finally going to become a reality. Even at a somewhat advanced age he was able to attend and judge for the first Americal Kennel Club lure coursing trial held in Hanover, Pennsylvania on August 31, 1991.

RACING AWARDS

Lyle had to be proud that the sport he initiated, with only a handful of people and a lot of enthusiasm, had grown in twenty years to a sport approved and adopted by the American Kennel Club. His beloved Borzois and all sighthounds could now earn their titles approved by the ADC. These titles are:

JUNIOR COURSER: A hound earns this title by completing a 600 yard course with a minimum of four turns.

SENIOR COURSER: A hound earns this title by running with other hounds of the same breed but not interfering with them.

FIELD CHAMPION: The third title, when awarded, includes the competitive prefix of Field Champion (FC), which is earned by attaining fifteen points with two First placements. Each of the First placements must be for three or more points.

The American Sighthound Field Association awards two titles, those of F.CH. and LCM. Both of these titles appear after the hounds registered name. The Field Champion title is earned by attaining 100 points with two First placements or one First and two Second placedments. The Lure Courser of Merit title is awarded after a hound completes the requirements for the Field Champion title and accumulates another 300 points and an additional four First placements. The Lure Courser of Merit title can be duplicated as many times as possible, and the LCM behind the hound's name will appear as LCM II, LCM III, and so on.

The American Whippet Club has a National Point Racing programme, known as NPR. From successful participation in this programme, Whippets may gain their ARM title or that of Award of Racing Merit. This coveted title has been earned by less than 300 dogs to date. The programme was begun in 1967 and at present runs around 30 meets a year around the US and Canada.

THE COURSING WHIPPET

When lure coursing started in California, Whippets were ready, willing and able to compete. Whippets remain the most exciting of all of the sighthound breeds to watch lure coursing. This breed can boast the highest percentage of individuals that try lure coursing will lure course. Approximately ninety-five per cent of all Whippets will lure course, compared to forty or fifty per cent of some of the other sighthound breeds. Whippets also have the largest entries at Field Trials and the competition is always extremely keen.

The Whippet is an exciting coursing hound because of the five categories by which they are judged in lure coursing. The Whippet is top in several areas and near the top in the others. Enthusiasm is the Whippet's forté. They possess more enthusiasm for the chase that the other breeds. This enthusiasm carries over into all the other categories making the Whippet always exciting to watch, especially as they dive for, and often catch the lure, in a spectacular head over heels tumble.

Follow is the next judging category, and most Whippets follow like little slot cars on a track. Some of the more seassoned LCM Whippets will cut a corner to run to a spot that they think the lure is going to go, but this usually only happens after many trials.

Although the Whippet is not the fastest of the sighthounds (with Greyhounds, Borzoi and Scottish Deerhounds holding this honour), the Whippet is the quickest, accelerating to full speed within only a few strides. Because of its light weight and muscle mass, the Whippet is the most agile of all the breeds, being able to zig and turn quickly in pursuit of the lure. Whippets run at 120 per cent capabilities all the time, and for this reason, do not possess great endurance. However, they quickly recover from the course and are able to compete in another course much faster than the other sighthound breeds.

Lure Coursing has certainly grown in leaps and bounds from its meagre beginnings in 1972, with only a few trials with a very limited entry. In 1993 there were in excess of 550 combined trials with total entries of over 20,000 hounds.

APPENDIX

GLOSSARY OF TERMS USED IN THE DOG WORLD

Angulation: The angle at which the joints fit into each other.
Apple-headed: The skull is domed.
Brisket: The front part of the chest below the neck, between the front legs.
Cat-feet: Short, round as in a cat's paw.
Chest: The front part of the body framework.
Cloddy: Low to the ground, too short on leg.
Cowhocks: The hock joint turns inwards to almost touch each other, causing the hind feet to point outward.
Dew Claws: Extra claws attached to legs above the feet. Sometimes on all four legs, but mainly on the front legs.
Dewlap: Loose pendulous skins on the throat.
Dish-faced: A hollow concave before the eye, forming a saucer-like depression between the tip of the nose and the forehead.
Down-faced: A completely level head from skull to nose, with no stop.
Down on pastern. Too much angle of the front feet, mostly a weakness.
Elbow: The joint at the top of the leg where the front leg joins the lower part of the shoulder blade.
Flews: Overhanging top lips.
Foreface: The part of the head in front of the stop.
Haw: The red inside eyelid.
Height: The dog measured from shoulder (withers) to the ground.
Hock: The joint between the foot and the upper part or thigh of the hindleg.
Level mouth: Term applied to a dog whose teeth meet evenly.
Loin: The lower part of the body between the last rib and the hip joint.
Low-set: The base of the tail is not on the level of the back.
Occiput. The prominent raised bone at the back of the skull.
Overshot: Where the top teeth project well over the bottom teeth.

Pastern: The part of the front leg from the knee joint to the foot.

Racy: Too slight in build with no substance.

Roachback: A convex curvature of the back.

Short-coupled: Short between the last rib and the hip joint, causing too short in loin.

Shoulder: The area on the back line at base of neck.

Snipey: Muzzle tapering too much instead of a filled in under jaw.

Splay foot: Foot spreading too long, toes not knuckled up.

Stifle: The joint on the inner side of a dog's hindleg.

Stop: The depression in front of the eyes between the forehead and the upper part of the muzzle.

Tuck-up: Too drawn up at the belly.

Withers: The space between the shoulder blades at the base of the neck.